Schooners, Skiffs & Steamships

Stories along Lake Superior's Water Trails

Schooners, Skiffs & Steamships

Stories along Lake Superior's Water Trails

Paintings and Companion Stories by Howard Sivertson

Lake Superior Port Cities Inc.
Duluth, Minnesota
2001

First edition published August 2001 by

 LAKE SUPERIOR PORT CITIES INC.
P.O. Box 16417
Duluth, Minnesota 55816-0417
USA
888-BIG LAKE (244-5253) • www.lakesuperior.com
Publishers of *Lake Superior Magazine* and *Lake Superior Travel Guide*

5 4 3 2 1

Library of Congress Cataloging-In-Publication Data

Sivertson, Howard, 1930-
    Schooners, skiff & steamships : stories along Lake Superior's water trails : paintings and companion stories / by Howard Sivertson.
        p. cm.
    Includes bibliographical references.
    ISBN 0-942235-51-7
    1. Frontier and pioneer life – Superior, Lake, Region – Anecdotes. 2. Frontier and pioneer life – Superior, Lake, Region – Pictorial works. 3. Superior, Lake, Region – History – Anecdotes. 4. Superior, Lake, Region – History – Pictorial works. 5. Waterways – Superior, Lake, Region – History – Anecdotes. 6. Waterways – Superior, Lake, Region – History – Pictorial works. 7. Pioneers – Superior, Lake, Region – History – Anecdotes. 8. Pioneers – Superior, Lake, Region – History – Pictorial works. 9. Boats and boating – Superior, Lake, Region – History – Anecdotes. 10. Boats and boating – Superior, Lake, Region – History – Pictorial works. I. Title: Schooners, skiffs, and steamships. II Title.
F552 .S57 2001
977.4'9 – dc21   2001042724

Printed in Canada

   Editors: Paul L. Hayden, Hugh E. Bishop, Konnie LeMay
   Designs: Mathew Pawlak, Erica Nord
   Printer: Friesen Book Division, Winnipeg, Manitoba

This book is dedicated to
Myrtle and Art Sivertson's family and descendants.

Ontario   Nipigon

                                                                    N
                                                                  W ⊕ E
                                                                    S
                                              Ontario

Kam River   Pic River
Port Arthur
                        Thunder
Fort William   Bay

Boundary Waters   Pigeon River   Pie Island   Lake
                              McKellar   Superior
Grand Portage   Point
                            Isle Royale   Michipicoten
Grand Marais

Minnesota   Michipicoten Island
       Lutsen
       Tofte   Eagle River   Copper Harbor

Beaver Bay   Montreal River

Two Harbors   Hancock
                        Houghton
Duluth
          Bayfield   Whitefish Point
Superior Washburn   La Pointe   Ontonagon
City   Brule   L'Anse
        River   Ashland   Pointe Aux Pins
                              Marquette   Sault Ste. Marie
     Wisconsin   Munising   Michigan

Table of Contents

Acknowledgments

A special thanks to Dr. Timothy Cochrane for providing me access to his research effort regarding the journals of the Hudson's Bay Company at Fort William and the letters of early Jesuit priests of western Lake Superior.

A special thanks also to my lifelong friend Donn Larson for writing the Afterward and for his editorial expertise needed to make my text more presentable to the critical eyes of the likes of Miss Snodgrass, whose class in English Donn and I shared at Denfeld High School in 1946.

Thanks also to:

Arrowhead Library System
Jim Brandenburg
Bobby Don Brazell
Cook County Historical Society
Carol Desain
Grand Portage National Monument
Thom Holden
Isle Royale National Park Service
Isle Royale Natural History Association
Jesuit Letters
Ted Johnson
Pat Labadie
Lake County Historical Society

Lake Superior Magazine
Old Fort William Librarians
Bill Peterson
Dr. Willis Raff
St. Louis County Historical Society
Tom Seymour
Arthur Sivertson
Elaine Sivertson
Jan Sivertson
Jeff Sivertson
Liz Sivertson
Stanley Sivertson
Thunder Bay Historical Museum
Brian Tofte

Preface

It would be impossible to tell the story of the discovery, settlement and economic growth of Lake Superior's communities without referring to the many interesting watercraft that carried our ancestors. From the bark canoes and wooden schooners that transported the fur trade and the Mackinaw boats, skiffs and bateaux that worked her shores to the first side-wheel and propeller-driven steamships that hauled passengers and freight, Lake Superior's early settlers relied on water transportation as a lifeline to civilization.

I was surprised when my editor informed me that my new book is about boats. My purpose for painting the pictures and writing the stories was to illustrate interesting, colorful stories about the *people* who discovered and settled this area. It just happened that watercraft were the most common denominator that connected the tales.

Most of the schooners and ships with names have never been seen before my paintings brought them to life, nor have any of the historical events in the book been visually documented before, to my knowledge.

So, welcome to *Schooners, Skiffs & Steamships*, a story of people surviving on Lake Superior's water trails.

– Howard Sivertson

Introduction

Snow fell gently on the frozen Boundary Waters lake, covering it with a thick blanket that absorbed every sound. The soft woosh of a whiskey jack's wings startled me as it glided past my ear to inspect my open packsack. My fishing hole was in sharp contrast against the flat, seemingly endless expanse of white that showed no contours. The muffled sounds of ravens playing overhead and my own rummaging, setting up to fish, were the loudest sounds I'd heard since I left my truck at the end of the Gunflint Trail.

This must be the way it sounded throughout the North American wilderness before the white man's noisy intrusion. Before he brought his blunderbusses and cannons there was very little noise other than natural sounds to disturb the tranquility. Hunting with bows and arrows, fishing out of bark canoes, making maple sugar and harvesting wild rice were silent activities. Even wooden hoes cultivating potato patches made little noise. Snow crunching underfoot, bird songs, children playing and the occasional yelp of a dog were only slight intrusions onto the vast silence of their environment.

Even after white people arrived in the Lake Superior area, it remained relatively quiet – except for muskets, cannon and chansons – until the mid-1800s. Steam engines broke the silence on the big lake in the 1840s when the steamships *Independence* and *Napoleon* rumbled about the lake at four miles per hour, spewing billows of black smoke from their stacks, laying a blanket of soot to smudge the skyline. The unearthly sounds of the monstrous ships were, to say the least, unsettling to some Native Americans. The roaring scream of the steam whistles frightened them half to death. But it was just a hint of the din to come when the country entered the industrial/machine age after the turn of the century. The natural world and the tribal way of life began to suffer dearly from white men's "progress."

Before 1900, even the white settler died in the same era he was born. Grandchildren used the same tools, used the same horse power, sang the same songs and danced to the same music as their grandparents. The term "generation gap" had yet to be invented.

Since the beginning of our presence on earth until the advent of railroads, we never traveled faster than a horse could carry us – about 32 miles per hour. By the mid-1900s, we were traveling faster than the speed of sound. It seems to me that noise levels increase in direct proportion to the speed we travel.

Walking was the most common mode of transportation before the machine age. Early explorers and surveyors walked thousands of miles across Canadian and American territories. Native people walked all over North America on annual migrations and trading trips. Pioneers walked from Missouri to Oregon and California. Civil War veterans journeyed thousands of miles on foot to return home after the war. Jesuit priests snowshoed and paddled canoes around Lake Superior to tend their flocks. Walking the old military road from St. Paul to Superior City at the head of Lake Superior was common for early settlers, who traveled in midwinter with just a long coat, blanket roll and a loaf of bread. Walking to Duluth from Grand Marais on the frozen lake was necessary for pioneers who had to conduct business in the city during the winter. Good or bad, every day must have been an adventure.

America's frontier moved west in the 19th century following the pathways of Lewis and Clark, Zebulon Pike and John Fremont to the West Coast and Southwest Territories. In Lake Superior country, voyageurs, tribal people and fur traders were still paddling bark canoes from Grand Portage and then Fort William to the Canadian Northwest. Explorers like Alexander Mackenzie, Simon Frazer and David Thompson were passing through Grand Portage and Fort William to explore, survey and map all of Canada from the Arctic Circle to the Pacific Ocean. They blazed trails that immigrants would follow in years to come.

Commerce on Lake Superior was interrupted for a few years during the War of 1812, when North West Company ships were either captured, destroyed or forced into hiding by American ships. John Jacob Astor, by this time, had expanded operations of his American Fur Company to Fort Astoria at the mouth of the Columbia River in the Northwestern United States in an attempt to keep the North West Company from trading in the new American territories.

The survey that established the border between United States and Canadian territories was finally completed and mapped by David Thompson in 1816. Just a few years later, in 1823-25, an English Navy lieutenant, Henry Wolsey Bayfield, surveyed and charted Lake Superior waters using the Hudson's Bay Company schooner *Recovery* out of Fort William as his base of operation. After the *Recovery II* was sent to the lower lakes in 1828, there were no large schooners on Lake Superior until 1835, when Ramsay Crooks of the American Fur Company had the 112-ton schooner *John Jacob Astor* built at Pointe Aux Pins, near Sault Ste. Marie, Ontario. The Hudson's Bay schooner *Whitefish* and American Fur's *William Brewster* joined the *Astor* shortly thereafter.

Meanwhile back on the frontier west and south of Lake Superior, the natives were still too restless to permit white settlers to move onto the land. Expeditions by Lewis Cass and Henry Schoolcraft in the 1820s and '30s helped to bring peace to the area, while inoculating thousands of tribal people against small pox. Treaties with the tribes were signed in the 1830s, '40s and '50s, making white settlement legal and safe.

Fur trading throughout the U.S. and Canada was failing as a viable industry. Furs became scarce and the market was poor. Out west in the Rockies, famed mountain men like Jim Bridger and Jedediah Smith came down out of the high country to become guides of the expeditions and wagon trains on their way to California and Oregon. Back on Lake Superior, Ramsay Crooks of the American Fur Company reacted to the defunct fur trade by directing his company's energy into harvesting the unlimited supply of the Lake Superior's fish to sell to markets in the east and south. With headquarters at La Pointe in the Apostle Islands, Crooks established fish camps along the lakeshore and at Isle Royale. The Hudson's Bay Company followed suit by establishing the lake's second commercial fishery at Fort William. Commercial fishing may not have been as exciting as the battle Jim Bowie and Davy Crockett were fighting at the Alamo for Texas independence at the time. The depression of 1836 that caused the American Fur Company to fail by 1842 must have seemed almost as exciting to Ramsay Crooks and crew.

The schooner *Astor* sank in a storm at Copper Harbor and the *Brewster* went to Detroit after the bankruptcy, leaving the sails of only the schooners *Whitefish* and *Algonquin* to break Lake Superior's horizon for several years.

Pioneers were starting to move west in wagon trains along the Oregon and California Trails. Brigham Young brought the Mormons to Salt Lake City. Presbyterian, Methodist and Catholic missionaries headed west with the wagons to Christianize the native people and start new churches among the settlements. While wagons carried missionaries west, bark canoes carried

Lake Superior missionaries to the Apostle Islands and beyond. Protestant missionaries Sherman Hall and William Boutwell had preceded Jesuit priest Father Frederic Baraga to La Pointe by several years when he arrived in 1835 on the maiden voyage of the schooner *Astor*. More priests would follow in a few years in an attempt to bring Christianity to the tribal people, with hopes of "civilizing" them to accept agrarian pursuits instead of their traditional hunter/gatherer ways.

More Jesuit priests arrived in western Lake Superior by the 1850s. Fathers Otto Skolla, Franz Pierz, Nicolas Frémiot, Dominic du Ranquet and others started missions at Pigeon River, Fort William and Grand Portage to serve the vast area from Grand Marais and Isle Royale to Lake Nipigon and Rainy Lake. Although none was massacred by the natives, as was the family of missionary Marcus Whiteman in Oregon, their hair-raising adventures while traveling on snowshoes, in canoes and small boats in all kinds of weather to serve their widely scattered congregations would fill many volumes.

Discoveries of copper and iron ore deposits by Dr. Douglass Houghton and others started the first mineral rush in the United States, preceding the Gold Rush in California by several years. Mining locations established at Isle Royale and Lake Superior's south shore attracted several small schooners, hauled over the portage at Sault Ste. Marie, to serve the anticipated boomtowns sure to grow around the lake. By 1848, Lake Superior was sporting two large steamships driven by the new propeller technology that would dominate shipping between lake ports. As slow and awkward as they were, the *Napoleon* and *Independence* were able to maintain relatively reliable schedules, since they didn't depend on which way the wind blew.

Shipping on Lake Superior increased sharply when the new locks at Sault Ste. Marie opened in 1855. Sidewheel steamer *Illinois* led the way for other steamers that carried passengers with all their earthly goods to settle the frontiers around the lake and beyond. A growing fleet of large sailing schooners became the workhorses of the lake, relegated to hauling copper, iron ore, lumber and freight. Except for an occasional Ojibway war party traveling south to harass the Sioux, and the growing tensions between North and South, life was relatively peaceful in Lake Superior country.

A resurgence of commerce and flow of settlers after the Civil War were encouraged by the completion of the Central and Union Pacific railroad to California. White man's grab for tribal lands created headlines, featuring names like General George Armstrong Custer, Chief Sitting Bull, Rosebud Creek and the Little Big Horn. People like Billy the Kid, Jesse James, Wyatt Earp, Cole Younger, William Quantrill and Kit Carson captured headlines with daring deeds that would become the basis for America's most popular mythology, "Cowboys and Indians."

Our heroes along Lake Superior's frontier were not as famous and did not make many headlines but were just as rough and rugged. John Beargrease was not as well known as Sitting Bull — except to people along his mail route waiting for his rowboat or dog team to bring them news from the old country. The Tofte brothers were no match for the Younger brothers when it came to making headlines, yet they founded a town and fished the dangerous waters of Lake Superior for several generations. The Weiland boys, unlike the James boys, lived honest, productive lives and earned fame along the shore as the first settlers to arrive on the steamship *Illinois,* to be cast ashore at the Beaver River with all their worldly belongings. They clung to the rugged coastline until their roots took hold. Their lumber mill furnished enough materials to build several towns along Lake Superior's coast.

The first folks to arrive along the north shore after the Treaty of 1854 were prospectors for gold, silver, copper and iron ore.

Most were disappointed and moved on, while a few decided to stay on as trappers, loggers, fishermen and farmers. After the Civil War, immigrants from Norway, Sweden, Finland and Denmark, searching for a land that looked like home where they could continue their traditions of fishing and farming, settled on the shore and built the towns of Two Harbors, Beaver Bay, Schroeder, Tofte, Lutsen, Grand Marais and Parkerville.

In the early days, mail and freight were delivered along the shore from Duluth to Fort William and Isle Royale by rowboats and dog teams. By the 1870s, steam tugs like the *T.H. Camp* and schooners like the *Stranger* delivered freight and picked up fish. Up until the 1920s there were no roads along the north shore, so most of the freight and passengers were delivered by water on ships such as the SS *Hiram Dixon* in the late 1800s and the SS *America*. After the *America* sank in 1928, freight, passengers and mail were shipped on trucks along the new Highway 61, putting an end to the need for large steamships along the shore. The *Winyah* and then the smaller *Detroit* ended the era of colorful steamship traffic along the shore and Isle Royale by 1952.

I enjoy trying to imagine living in the 19th century in a quiet world without machinery noises, electricity, photography, telephones, radio, TV, automobiles, airplanes, computers, VCRs and nuclear power. Before photography was invented in the mid-1800s, no one had ever seen pictures of their ancestors or relatives, no family albums, no baby pictures or pictures of family events, historic happenings or far-off places and people. They knew what the world looked like only by what they saw with their own eyes or by some artist's renderings, which may have been accurate or not.

The lack of photographic images made research difficult for many of the paintings in this book. I had to rely on verbal descriptions or artist interpretations at the time. My painting technique is a combination of the luminists and impressionists of the 19th century, which is fitting for the subjects of that era. I hope you find beauty and entertainment along with historical information concerning those colorful years along Lake Superior's frontier. These paintings are the only visual documentation that exists, to my knowledge, for most of the stories in this book.

– Howard Sivertson
Grand Marais, Minnesota
August 2001

Athabaska Brigade At Little Rock Portage

Winters were unbearably long and monotonous for employees of the North West Company stationed at isolated fur trading posts scattered throughout northwestern Canada in the late 1700s. They felt self-banished in the dreary bush country far from everything they held dear. By late winter, they tired of the cold, boredom and limited provisions that threatened their very existence. No wonder they longed for the good food, camaraderie, wine and wild parties at the Grand Portage Rendezvous each summer. There, on the shore of Lake Superior, the traders exchanged bales of furs collected from northern Indian hunters for the trade goods and supplies from Montreal necessary to survive and conduct business for another year.

The desire to attend Rendezvous at Grand Portage surmounted by far the pain of getting there. Carrying tons of furs over mosquito-infested portages and paddling heavily loaded bark canoes 18 hours a day for six weeks over a 4,000-mile round trip must have been worth the fun and games at Rendezvous. Then, after a few wild days of celebration, they returned via the same route loaded with tons of supplies and trade goods to face another long and lonesome winter in the bush.

Of the many canoes traveling to Grand Portage from posts scattered throughout northwest Canada, the brigade from Fort Chipewyan on Lake Athabaska traveled the farthest. Consequently, they were the last to arrive at Rendezvous and the first to leave.

The Athabaskan canoes left Lake Athabaska as soon as the rivers and lakes started breaking up in mid-May. Several 25-foot north canoes, loaded with more than 2,000 pounds of furs each, started the long journey south with six to eight voyageurs paddling each canoe.

From the Athabaska River they took the Clearwater River to the 13-mile Meythe Portage to Lac Ile-A-La-Crosse and the Churchill River. Canoes from other trading posts along the way joined the high spirited brigade en route to Rendezvous. From the Churchill River to Cumberland House, Sturgeon Weir River, Saskatchewan River and Lake Winnipeg, they entered the Boundary Waters chain that led to Fort Charlotte on the upper end of the Pigeon River and the Grand Portage. From Fort Charlotte it was a downhill walk across the nine-mile portage, with nothing to carry but their personal belongings and high expectations.

The canoes were left at Fort Charlotte, where trading post employees would repair them for the return trip north. The 90-pound packs of furs were left there also, to be carried across the portage by the lowly "porkeaters," young seasonal voyageurs from Montreal.

The business and revelry of the Athabaskans had to be accomplished quickly in order for them to leave in time to make it back to Fort Chipewyan before the far north waterway froze. After a few years, a special trading depot named Athabaska House was built on Rainy Lake, making the trip shorter, less dangerous but probably less entertaining.

The painting is my interpretation of how the Athabaska Brigade may have looked arriving at Little Rock Portage, just off Gunflint Lake, on its return trip from Rendezvous to Lake Athabaska.

Brigade Departing Little Rock Portage

The Party's over. The business done. Time for the Northwesters to return to wintering posts before winter freezes their water highways. Canoes from Athabaska leave Rendezvous at Grand Portage first. Then those from Peace River, Saskatchewan River, Assinaboin River and all the posts in between, leaving at two-day intervals so as not to clog the portages and get the cargoes of supplies and trade goods mixed up. On Lake Superior, Montreal canoes filled with furs head back to the St. Lawrence River in hopes of arriving in time to ship their precious cargo to England before freeze-up.

I imagine the return trip for the northmen was not as high-spirited as the voyage to Rendezvous. But depression didn't last long among the playful voyageurs, who instinctively knew how to get the most fun and pleasure out of each day, no matter where they were. Their love for singing, mischievousness and playing games is legendary. Canoe races en route helped lessen the tedium of paddling. One canoe race up Lake Winnipeg was recorded to have lasted 48 hours without a break.

Portages along the way ranged anywhere from a few yards, like the Little Rock Portage on the Granite River, to the 13-mile Meythe Portage between Lac-Ile-A-La-Crosse and Clearwater River. Bark canoes were carried in an upright position on the shoulders of two voyageurs to the other side of the portage and put in the water. Trade goods and supplies were toted in 180-pound loads on the backs of voyageurs and reloaded in waiting canoes.

Native Americans established the routes that the voyageurs used long before they arrived and continued using them long after they were gone. At times, native families traveled with the voyageur brigades to trade or visit relatives. I included a 3-fathom native canoe, shown nearest the falls, that could be on its way from Montreal to the Peace River or any points in between. Native people were at home wherever they happened to be in their frequent wandering from the Rocky Mountains and Arctic Circle to the Ohio River Valley, Eastern Canada or Mississippi River Valley – unless, of course, they happened to be at war with other tribes in certain areas.

The voyageurs loading their canoes for Athabaska or other trading posts in Northwest Canada had to travel on tight schedules to arrive before freeze-up. Unlike the native people, they were not at home anywhere, except at their assigned destination, and would probably not survive the deadly winter if they failed to arrive on time.

North by Northwest to the Pacific

Grand Portage and then Fort William were not only the hinge pins of fur trade in North America, they were headquarters and jumping off places for some of the great explorers of the Northwest.

David Thompson headquartered at Fort William during his lengthy survey trips throughout Canada in the early 1800s. Lieutenant Henry Wolsey Bayfield surveyed Lake Superior from Fort William from 1823 to 1825.

Alexander Mackenzie traveled through Grand Portage to Lake Athabaska several times on his way to discovering the Mackenzie River in 1789 and his route to the Pacific Ocean in 1793.

Inspired by Peter Pond, a fellow fur trader of the North West Company at Fort Chipewyan on Lake Athabaska, Mackenzie laid plans to find a trade route to the Pacific Ocean. Lured on by a crude, inaccurate map drawn by Pond that showed the Pacific Ocean much closer and more easily accessible than it was, Mackenzie enthusiastically set forth from Fort Chipewyan to lead a group of voyageurs north through the Slave Lake region. But the river he hoped would lead him to the Pacific swung due north sweeping Mackenzie into the tide waters of the Arctic Ocean. Even though his discovery and exploration of the Mackenzie River was a great achievement, Mackenzie was disappointed in not achieving his original goal.

He did not remain discouraged long and soon laid plans for another attempt to find a trade route to the Pacific. Mackenzie went back to England for one year to study and improve his geographic knowledge and navigational skills. On his return trip he once again paddled to Grand Portage and up the Boundary Water route that eventually took him back to Fort Chipewyan on Lake Athabaska. In 1792, he led his group of explorers in a canoe across Canada to the Peace River then down the Parsnip River, across the Rocky Mountains to a tributary of the Frazer River and finally salt water.

Raging rapids, smashed canoes, lost ammunition and supplies, hostile tribes, freezing blizzards and starvation were just some of the hazards that the Mackenzie group had to overcome on their way to finally discovering a route to the Pacific. Without the help of friendly members of the Bella Coola tribe, they would have perished. After inscribing a large rock with the message: "Alex Mackenzie from Canada by land July 1793," Mackenzie returned to Fort Chipewyan from his 3,000-mile round trip on August 24, 1793.

New Year's Eve at the Mouth of the Pigeon River – 1800

A dram of grog to voyageur employees of the North West Company was a tradition on New Year's throughout the fur trade. A regale of rum was a welcome treat that helped break the monotony of long winter days at lonely fur trading posts scattered throughout the northwest. And so it probably was for the crew aboard the company schooner *Otter*, hauled out for repairs at the mouth of the Pigeon River in 1800.

Throughout the lonely winter they were isolated from their nearest companions, who were manning the almost deserted trading post at Grand Portage, Minnesota, more than 12 miles away by water. Only an occasional visit by the Ojibway hunter who supplied the crew with venison broke the monotony.

Captain Maxwell of the *Otter* received orders in August 1800 to haul out and repair the prematurely rotting vessel that winter. Built at Pointe aux Pins just north of Sault Ste. Marie in 1793 to haul company supplies on Lake Superior, the 75-ton schooner was already in need of major repairs.

"St. Maries, 26 Augt., 1800

"Captain Maxwell,

"As soon as convenient after unloading your cargo at Grand Portage, you will proceed to the Riviere aux Tourtres (Pigeon River) where the vessel is to winter. In regard to her repairs, by your own imagination, you will best know what she requires. Anything that is rotten or split must be removed."

Captain Maxwell was further instructed to "not undo more than you can replace before spring, for nothing must prevent your leaving Portage (for the Sault) the first week in May.

"I have agreed with two men at the Grand Portage to provide you with 16 or 20 barrels of salt fish. Mr. Kenneth will make a fair division of the potatoes between your people and the men at the fort, after laying a part of the quantity necessary for seed and for the table next summer. But as quantity cannot be great, you must deal them out sparingly and in issuing the provisions to your men, you ought to follow the example of the fort, giving it every two days – dividing the fish and corn as regular as you can. You will take 36 bushels at the Grand Portage. According to my calculations this will be sufficient – but you can easily calculate with Mr. McKenzie and if more is required you can take it, of course.

"You will be allowed rum to give them a glass of grog now and then when they work well, and you can take a couple bags of flour for their use to give them at times when you think necessary."

The letter goes on to grant Captain Maxwell for his own use: a keg of butter, a keg of wine, three bags of flour, 100 pounds of sugar and any meat brought in by the Ojibway hunters (which I assume was to be shared with the crew). He was also ordered to build a large bateaux for unloading the *Otter* at the Sault.

Maybe on that New Year's Eve in 1800, the visiting Ojibway men brought venison for the crew and they all shared a bit of grog in celebration not only for the coming New Year, but also for a welcome change in their salt fish diet.

Charting Lake Superior – 1823-1825

Early fur traders, explorers and missionaries found their way across the wilderness of North America by following primitive maps drawn on birch bark by native guides. They in turn drew their own crude maps for others to follow. Although somewhat more accurate than the bark scribblings, they were still too inaccurate to define exact locations of trading posts or boundary lines.

At the end of the American Revolution, the new boundary between the United States and Canada had to be surveyed and accurate maps were needed from the East Coast along the Great Lakes, Boundary Waters, Great Plains and across the Rockies to the Columbia River and Pacific Ocean. Charting the St. Lawrence River and the Great Lakes was also important for political and navigational purposes.

Onetime Hudson's Bay Company fur trader, explorer and surveyor David Thompson was hired by the North West Company to survey and locate precisely, on accurate maps, the locations of their many trading posts in Canada. He spent many years traveling more than 12,000 miles in canoes, on foot and snowshoes, from his headquarters at Fort William to the Columbia River and the Pacific. Many of those miles he bush-whacked accompanied by his wife and small children. Besides establishing trading post locations, he made the first accurate maps of most of the boundary between Canada and the U.S.

As Thompson was the premiere map maker of Canada, so was Lieutenant Henry Wolsey Bayfield of the British Royal Navy the premiere chart maker of the Great Lakes.

Born in 1795 in England, Bayfield joined the Royal Navy at age 11 and fought in the naval battle of Gibraltar in 1806. It was the same year that Lewis and Clark returned from their famed "Voyage of Discovery" across North America. At age 22, Bayfield was placed in charge of surveying lakes Erie and Huron, where he charted coastlines and more than 20,000 islands. He worked out of two rowboats for four years, sleeping under sailcloth and buffalo hides at night.

In 1823, his survey continued on Lake Superior on board the Hudson's Bay Company schooner *Recovery* based at Fort William. Leased from the company by the British Admiralty, the 90-ton schooner was Bayfield's floating headquarters for the 1823 season, after which the badly rotting hull was cut up for firewood.

Bayfield transferred his headquarters to the brand new Hudson's Bay Company schooner *Recovery II* until 1825, when the survey was completed. In 1828, the 133-ton schooner sailed to the lower lakes and was sold.

The painting shows the *Recovery* anchored along the north shore, while Bayfield sets out for a day of surveying and sounding, still working out of a small boat that he preferred for efficiency and maneuverability.

Bayfield retired as an admiral in 1867, after accomplishing the astounding feat of surveying, sounding and charting the thousands of miles of shoreline, many thousands of reefs and more than 20,000 islands of Lake Superior, Lake Huron, Lake Erie, St. Lawrence River, Nova Scotia, Labrador and Newfoundland.

Schoolcraft Expedition of 1832

In 1832, Lake Superior's horizon lay unbroken by masts and sails of the fur trade schooners of the 1820s. Schooners *John Jacob Astor* and *William Brewster* wouldn't be seen for another three years, when the American Fur Company would start its fisheries around the big lake's shores.

Only bark canoes and small Mackinaw barges hugged Lake Superior's shoreline on their seasonal errands, carrying a few furs, supplies and employees for the dwindling fur trade. The Lake Superior region was resting, getting its second wind in preparation for a new boom of activity.

An onslaught of miners, settlers, fishermen, loggers and merchants lay just beyond that unbroken horizon, waiting for treaties that would open new lands for Euro-American exploitation.

But first, in the eyes of the expansionists, the new frontier had to be explored and mapped. The Sioux and Chippewa had to discontinue their tribal warfare to make the frontier safe for settlement and commerce. Smallpox had to be brought under control and the various Indian tribes introduced to Christianity.

Henry Rowe Schoolcraft began his expedition in 1832 to the new frontier, west and south of Lake Superior, to accomplish these tasks. His expedition was authorized by the U.S. Office of Indian Affairs, counting on Schoolcraft's diplomatic skills to make peace among the warring tribes. Young geologist, biologist and physician Douglass Houghton vaccinated more than 2,000 Native Americans for smallpox and brought back samples of minerals, flora and fauna found along the way. Reverend William Boutwell tried to acquaint the native people with Christianity, but found the challenge extremely frustrating for lack of communication skills, even with the help of the expedition's interpreter, George Johnson.

The guardians of the expedition were Lieutenant James Allen and 10 soldiers from Fort Brady at Sault Ste. Marie. Lieutenant Allen, also the map maker of the expedition, accurately depicted the topography and waterways along their route from Fond du Lac (near western Duluth) to Lake Itasca, down the Mississippi to Fort Snelling, then north up the St. Croix and down the Brule River to Lake Superior.

Twenty mixed-blood voyageurs assumed the job of paddling and carrying tons of equipment and supplies for 2,800 miles and 80 days.

Schoolcraft's expedition left Sault Ste. Marie on June 7, 1832, with a flotilla similar to my interpretation in the painting. In the large bark canoe that led the group were Henry Schoolcraft, Douglass Houghton and eight voyageurs.

Reverend Boutwell, interpreter George Johnson, 12 voyageurs and most of the supplies occupied the large Mackinaw schooner-barge.

Lagging behind, as was to be the case during the entire journey, were the protectors of the expedition in a smaller Mackinaw schooner-barge. Lieutenant Allen and soldiers, unaccustomed to seafaring, fell far behind the more experienced voyageurs, who were experts in handling boats and canoes. Throughout the expedition, the soldiers seemed more concerned with catching up to food and supplies carried in the lead canoes than with the threat of hostile tribes.

Schoolcraft Expedition at the Mouth of the Brule River – August 5, 1832

The grueling tasks of Henry Rowe Schoolcraft's expedition in 1832 began as they ascended the portage around the rapids at the mouth of the St. Louis River. Here at Fond du Lac, they traded their large boats and canoe for smaller canoes and hired several Indian guides for the westward journey to the Mississippi River. After discovering the source of that river – a personal mission of Schoolcraft – they paddled downstream to Fort Snelling then up the St. Croix to the Brule River, returning to Lake Superior.

By the time the Schoolcraft expedition arrived at the mouth of the Brule, it could boast of a successful journey. Ojibway and Sioux tribes promised to stop warring. More than 2,000 people of those two tribes were vaccinated against smallpox. Samples of flora, fauna and minerals were secured, accurate maps were sketched and Lake Itasca was named as the true source of the Mississippi River.

Schoolcraft and the Reverend William Boutwell, who had led the expedition the entire journey, arrived at the mouth of the Brule River late Saturday evening, August 4, 1832. Douglass Houghton arrived the next morning, but Lieutenant James Allen and troops did not arrive until several days later. The trip up the St. Croix and down the Brule was extremely grueling for the men and disastrous for the frail bark canoes that had to be constantly repaired en route.

Imagine the relief they felt upon leaving the hot, mosquito-infested interior. Half starved, bruised and broken bodies felt the fresh cool breeze off Lake Superior as they coasted their battered, leaking canoes toward the sandbar at the river mouth.

Several lodges of the Fond du Lac tribe were encamped at the mouth, their summer fishery. They presented the ragged survivors with fresh-caught whitefish and trout while Schoolcraft distributed gifts to tribal leaders. An Ojibway named Mongozoid, who was given charge of Lieutenant Allen's Mackinaw boat, had it rigged and ready to go as promised.

It was the Sabbath and time to rest. Strong winds, partly sunny skies and occasional showers refreshed the men and revived their spirits. Canoes were mended, bodies scrubbed, fed and rested in preparation for the last leg of the trip home.

Without waiting for Lieutenant Allen and troops to arrive at the mouth, Schoolcraft, Boutwell and Houghton left for La Pointe where Boutwell stayed to build his church. Schoolcraft departed immediately for Sault Ste. Marie by canoe. Houghton waited at La Pointe to rendezvous with Allen, who finally arrived five days later – the first they'd seen of him since the St. Croix River. All parties except for Boutwell arrived at the Sault on August 25, 1832.

American Fur Company Schooner *John Jacob Astor*

After amalgamation of the North West Company with the Hudson's Bay Company in 1821, fur trade traffic on Lake Superior all but disappeared. The last of the large fur trade schooners left when the schooner *Recovery II* was sent to the lower lakes in 1829. Some large 36-foot bark canoes continued to haul Hudson's Bay Company officials between Sault Ste. Marie and Fort William until the 1880s. Small Mackinaw schooners still scooted from trading post to trading post attending to the dwindling fur trade business on Lake Superior. But the big sails were gone from the big lake until 1835, when the grand topsail schooner *John Jacob Astor* was launched at Pointe Aux Pins near the Sault.

Because of the failing fur trade, John Jacob Astor's American Fur Company was reorganized in the early 1830s, resulting in Ramsay Crooks becoming owner of the northern district that included Lake Superior. He turned his company's energy to harvesting the seemingly unlimited supply of lake trout and whitefish as a major new source of revenue. Fish camps were established along the south shore, north shore and Isle Royale, with headquarters at La Pointe in the Apostle Islands.

To handle the shipping of supplies and fish, he had the 112-ton schooner *John Jacob Astor* constructed in 1835. Captain Charles Stannard was its master until 1842. The fish business grew rapidly, but was limited by the *Astor*'s inability to serve all the fish camps often enough. A new schooner, *William Brewster*, was built to haul fish from the widely scattered fish camps to headquarter warehouses at La Pointe. This left the *John Jacob Astor* to concentrate on hauling fish and supplies between La Pointe and Sault Ste. Marie.

In 1839, the American Fur Company had two smaller schooners built to collect fish from around Isle Royale's camps. They delivered their cargoes to loading docks at the island's Rock Harbor and Siskiwit Bay to be picked up later by the *Brewster*.

Even though fishing was excellent, the financial panic from 1839 to 1841 put the promising new enterprise into bankruptcy. The schooner *Brewster* sailed to American Fur Company headquarters at Detroit in 1842. The *John Jacob Astor* sank in 1844 during a storm at Copper Harbor.

After the departure of American Fur Company ships on Lake Superior, the sails of the Hudson's Bay Company schooner *Whitefish*, hauling fish and supplies from Fort William to the Sault, were joined by the sails of the small schooner *Algonquin*, serving the infant mining industry just beginning to grow on Lake Superior.

Hudson's Bay Company Schooner *Whitefish* at Fort William – 1837-1852

After the adventurous, colorful, highly romanticized heyday of the fur trade in North America, the large trading companies went into decline and not much was recorded of those less glorious days. After the amalgamation of the North West Company with the Hudson's Bay Company in 1821, fur trade traffic was rerouted from Lake Superior to Hudson Bay. Fort William was no longer the major trading post and rendezvous point that it was from 1804 to 1821. Its destiny was to slowly fade into non-existence in a few years, except for a new idea spawned by their rival, the American Fur Company.

Both companies had harvested Lake Superior whitefish, trout and siscowets for many years to provide food for their employees. Then in 1835, Ramsay Crooks of the American Fur Company decided to establish a large commercial fishery to harvest the unlimited fish resource for profit.

Hudson's Bay Company at Fort William immediately followed suit and by 1837 built the 40-ton schooner *Whitefish* to haul the fish to market. It delivered supplies and salt to company posts at Michipicoten, Pic River and Fort William and returned with barrels of salt fish to Sault Ste. Marie.

Fishing stations were established from the Pigeon River to Black Bay, where hundreds of barrels of fish were caught and shipped to Fort William by company boats. Crews of Native American, Metis and French fishermen and their wives were sent to the stations each September through November to set nets.

Many barrels of salt fish were consumed by employees each winter, but the hundreds of barrels left over were shipped to market in the spring aboard the *Whitefish*.

The painting shows how *Whitefish* may have looked arriving at Fort William in 1850. I used artist William Napier's 1857 painting of the fort to represent how it may have appeared in those years. Governor Simpson visited occasionally in the 36-foot Montreal bark canoe that I include in the painting, along with a priest, possibly Father Frémiot, waiting on the dock. The bark wigwam is probably home to a freeman and his family, many of whom lived close to the fort, but were not under contract to the company. They are seasonal employees, but not *engagés*. Stockade walls are gone, maybe torn down for building material or firewood.

After serving the Hudson's Bay Company until 1852, *Whitefish* was replaced by the schooner *Isobel* or *Isabel*.

American Fur Company Schooner *William Brewster* – Grand Portage, 1839

Davy Crocket and Jim Bowie were fighting the Battle of the Alamo in Texas. Jim Bridger and the last of the mountain men left the fur trapping business to become wagon-train guides. Chief Ross led his Cherokee nation on "the trail of tears" from Georgia to Oklahoma. At this same time, Ramsay Crooks of the American Fur Company began the first commercial fishing enterprise on Lake Superior.

As the fur trade declined, Crooks, president of the New American Fur Company Lake Superior District, built fishing camps at L' Anse, Montreal River and Grand Marais in Michigan, Grand Portage on the north shore and Isle Royale, with company headquarters at La Pointe in the Apostle Islands. His fishermen employees were Native Americans, French, people of mixed blood and leftover voyageurs from the fur trade who set nets and hook-lines for lake trout, siscowet and whitefish.

We assume that fishermen used large bark canoes, Mackinaw schooners, various kinds of barges and bateaux in fishing waters adjacent to their camps. Two small sloops, *Madeline* and *Siskiwit*, collected fish, salted down in barrels, from fishing stations scattered around Isle Royale and deposited them at deep-water docks at Rock Harbor and Siskiwit Bay.

Ramsay Crooks had the 73-ton schooner *William Brewster* built at Pointe Aux Pins in 1838 to carry salt, supplies and barrels of salt fish between La Pointe and Isle Royale and north and south shore fishing camps. The painting shows how the *Brewster* may have looked approaching the company warehouse on Sheep Island in Grand Portage Bay in 1839. Captain John Wood was at the helm and Lake Superior district manager, Gabriel Franchere of Fort Astoria fame, was aboard to inspect the Grand Portage fish camp managed by Pierre Cote.

Ten fishermen and one cooper (for making barrels) were employed at the Grand Portage fishery that extended for 40 miles along the shore to Grand Marais. They would ship 300 to 400 barrels of salt fish each season aboard the *Brewster* for La Pointe.

Although fish production exceeded the expectations of Ramsay Crooks, the panic of 1837–1841 destroyed the market, causing the company to fail in 1842. The *Brewster* sailed to company headquarters at Detroit in 1842 where, we assume, it ended its days.

Douglass Houghton's Last Ride – Eagle River 1845

'Within 200 yards of shore we shipped another sea, which was followed by a larger billow, and the boat capsized with all hands under her," recalled Peter McFarland, one of the two survivors of the fatal shipwreck that took the lives of three passengers including Dr. Douglass Houghton. He continued: "Instantly a heavy sea struck the boat, throwing it perpendicularly into the air. It fell over backwards and Dr. Houghton disappeared forever."

On October 13, 1845, Dr. Houghton, state geologist for the new state of Michigan, along with four others in a Mackinaw boat trying to return to Eagle River, were caught in a northeast blizzard on Lake Superior and capsized. Voyageurs Pete McFarland, Tousin Piquette, Oliver Larimer and Babtiste Bodrie rowed while Dr. Houghton steered as they left the mining location of Hassey and Avery for Eagle River, five miles to the east.

They had just passed the last beach where they could have landed safely when the storm struck with all its fury. In desperation, Dr. Houghton steered through giant breakers in a fatal attempt to find refuge on the exposed rocky coast. Only Peter McFarland and Babtiste Bodrie were washed safely ashore. After searching for the others and about to freeze themselves, they walked through the snowstorm to Eagle River and survived. Douglass Houghton's body was found on a beach the following spring.

Dr. Houghton's skills as a physician, geologist, botanist and natural historian earned him a place in Henry Rowe Schoolcraft's two expeditions to the Mississippi River in 1831 and 1832, where he vaccinated more than 2,000 native people against small pox and brought back valuable mineral specimens found along the way. As a young man he surveyed both the Upper and Lower peninsulas of Michigan for future mining locations. His 1840 expedition along the south shore of Lake Superior and Isle Royale discovered vast stores of copper and iron ore that led to mining operations at Calumet, Negaunee and Isle Royale.

His explorations caused the first mineral rush in the United States, beating the Gold Rush in California by a year or so. Dr. Houghton's work, largely responsible for the birth of the mining industry in the Upper Peninsula and Isle Royale, was cut short by his untimely death.

Father Baraga's Miraculous Landing at Cross River in 1846

Jesuit priests found a hostile environment for teaching Christianity to tribal people along the shores of Lake Superior in the 1660s. After Father Marquette's retreat to Sault Ste. Marie in 1671, Catholic priests made no further attempts to Christianize the native people for 164 years. By 1835, when Father Frederic Baraga arrived at La Pointe in the Apostle Islands, the Sioux had been driven off by the Ojibway, the Henry Rowe Schoolcraft expeditions had laid the groundwork for peace between traditionally warring tribes and treaties between the United States and the Ojibway people had been signed.

The time seemed right and the choice of missionary was right. Bringing Christianity to the native bands around Lake Superior was definitely Father Baraga's calling. His toughness, resilience, perseverance and genuine love of the Native American people made his mission possible in the face of all odds. His unswerving faith seemingly accomplished miracles for him. His terrifying trip across Lake Superior is just one of the many miracles accomplished by his steadfast faith and a lot of hard rowing by his guide, Louis Gaudine.

Against the advice of his faithful guide and everyone gathered on shore, Baraga insisted on crossing the lake in a totally inadequate boat in the fall of 1846. Rather than taking the traditional route – following the shore line – he decided to sail his frail 18-foot skiff directly across the lake from Sand Island to the north shore, saving weeks of time and almost 100 miles. His mission to serve the people at Grand Portage seemed worthy of the risk.

With a light breeze in their favor and Louis at the oars, they made it halfway across before the storm out of the southwest hit them. While Gaudine struggled to row, Father Baraga sat in the bottom of the boat, seemingly oblivious to the rising wind and treacherous seas, reading aloud from his prayer book and offering encouraging words to Gaudine.

They approached the north shore, but Gaudine was exhausted and now faced a wall of pounding surf that threatened to keep them from landing. "Keep rowing straight ahead," commanded Baraga, who was now sitting up with tiller in hand as a giant sea lifted the small boat over a sandbar. It came to rest quietly in the calm waters of a river mouth.

Once safely ashore, Father Frederic Baraga and guide Louis Gaudine erected a cross and gave thanks for their safe arrival at what is now called the "Cross River."

Ojibway Family Netting Whitefish in Little Trout Bay

Archeologists tell us that prehistoric peoples harvested Lake Superior's fish more than 4,000 years ago. There is evidence that netting made of nettle bark was used by the Woodland People long before white men came to this area. Ojibway people have netted trout, whitefish and sturgeon along Lake Superior's shores from the 1500s and continue that tradition today.

Cotton nets probably superceded the nettle bark nets during the fur trade days. Linen net came along in the 1940s and today, nets made of monofilament catch the fish that feed us. Fishing canoes made of bark were used well into the late 1800s. Small bateau-like skiffs and Mackinaw boats gradually replaced the bark canoe starting in the 1820s or so.

Ojibway families fished primarily for subsistence. Jesuit priest Father Nicolas Frémiot wrote in his journal of 1851 that native families consumed anywhere from 12 to 25 barrels of salt fish per winter. At 200 pounds per barrel, the largest family could consume about 5,000 pounds. If the family had salt fish left over in the spring, it's quite likely they would trade it at trading posts for other necessities. The large majority of fish were netted in the fall, when trout and whitefish came into shallow water to spawn.

Jesuit journals or letters from the mid-1800s mention the Pakwadjinin family that set up a seasonal fish camp at Trout Bay, about five miles northeast of Pigeon Bay, each summer after collecting maple sugar inland. A large garden was planted with potatoes to provide the other half of their winter's diet. Louie Pakwadjinin would set nets to keep his family in fresh fish throughout the summer.

In the painting, I tried to capture the beauty and serenity of Pakwadjinin's surroundings, as he and his family lifted his nets in Little Trout Bay. Only the sounds of ravens or sea gulls broke the silence of the autumn day. One day he would see his first smudge of black smoke on the horizon and hear the first rumbling of giant engines pushing *Scootie-Nabbie-Quon* or other new propellers like the *Independence* or *Baltimore* bringing white men and their supplies and belongings to settle the shores that once were his people's.

Propeller *Independence* at Middle Island Passage

Its original claim to fame was being the first propeller-driven steamship on Lake Superior. It was also famous for having the first steam whistle on the big lake, used primarily to announce its arrival or departure and to frighten paddlers in small canoes.

It took seven weeks to drag the 118-foot, 280-ton ship *Independence* across the portage at Sault Ste. Marie in 1845 to begin a rather unglorious career hauling mail, passengers and freight between the infant ports along the south shore and Isle Royale. Unglorious because of the inordinate amount of time spent stranded and aground on Lake Superior's uncharted shoals, amounting to about a quarter of its time in service.

Its basic clipper-shaped hull, built in 1843, was well designed and pleasing to the eye. But in 1845, in an attempt to make an ocean-going craft for the European grain trade, another deck was added, topped off with passenger staterooms and pilothouse. Two rotary steam engines driving two propellers were installed, while still keeping a set of schooner-rigged sails for auxiliary power. Its top speed was hoped to be about eight miles per hour but only achieved a disappointing four. Too slow for its intended purpose, it was sold to S. McKnight, who hauled it over the portage to Lake Superior. Despite its unmaneuverability, caused by lack of speed and power and resulting in many hours aground, it was the undisputed queen of Lake Superior shipping. Its only competition was the small schooner *Algonquin* and several other schooners in the 40- to 60-ton class. Despite its awkwardness, it was a welcome sight when isolated folks saw its black smoke on the horizon and heard its rumbling engines and steam whistle announcing its long-awaited arrival.

The painting tries to capture the spirit of its arrival at Middle Island Passage to serve the mining community at Ransom townsite in Rock Harbor, Isle Royale. Catching sight of it from a long way off, Ojibway people, miners and fishermen race it to the dock in their canoes and Mackinaw boats to collect long awaited mail, groceries, supplies and passengers.

After serving Lake Superior's isolated communities for only eight years, the boilers of the *Independence* blew up just a mile from its dock at Sault Ste. Marie. Four people were killed, but the rest of its passengers and crew were rescued, floating on debris and hay bales being shipped to Ontonagon, on November 22, 1853.

INDEPENDENCE

H. SIVERTSON
©1999

Coming of the *Scootie-Nabbie-Quon* – 1848

Not much is known of the mysterious *Scootie-Nabbie-Quon,* as it was called by Ojibway people along Lake Superior's shores, many of whom ran in fear at the sight of the loud chugging, smoke-belching monster that they thought was towed through the water by giant sturgeons. The real name of the schooner was *Napoleon,* named after Emperor Napoleon Bonaparte of France. The Ojibway translation was how they heard "Schooner *Napoleon.*"

It began its shipping career on Lake Superior as a 180-ton sailing schooner launched at Sault Ste. Marie in 1845. Schooner *Napoleon* was converted to a steam-powered propeller-driven ship in 1848, making it one of the first ships on Lake Superior to take advantage of that new technology.

The propeller *Napoleon* chugged through the water at a top speed of four miles per hour – and that's with its auxiliary sails full of wind besides. Some passengers claimed it was so roly-poly in seas that its stacks scooped fish from the lake. But the Ojibway people had more to fear from it than its spooky appearance.

Hordes of newcomers were moving west to occupy tribal homelands. Mineral prospectors, miners, lumberjacks, fur traders, fishermen and settlers swarmed west aboard ships like *Napoleon.* Its decks were filled with immigrants and its holds filled with supplies bound for Marquette, Ontonagon, La Pointe, Superior City, Grand Portage and Isle Royale. In 1855, the new lock at Sault Ste. Marie would open its gates, releasing a flood of ships loaded with equipment and passengers to swell the burgeoning settlements around the lake.

An endless stream of white people would teem over the one-time Indian lands ceded to the United States and Canada by treaties, forcing the once-nomadic bands to be confined to reservations and to a lifestyle foreign to their natures.

But to the new arrivals, *Napoleon* and ships like it were taking them to the land of opportunity, the likes of which were unavailable to them in the old country. A new life of freedom and independence waited for them just over the horizon to the west. A rich land just waiting to be exploited.

While the *Scootie-Nabbie-Quon* was a symbol of despair and confinement to native peoples, the *Napoleon* symbolized hope and freedom to the Europeans.

Hudson's Bay Company Fishing Station at Pointe Au Père – circa 1850

Pointe Au Père was just one of several Hudson's Bay Company fishing stations among the islands and bays surrounding Fort William in the Thunder Bay area. Pointe Au Père was a regularly used campsite by early voyageur brigades going to and from Rendezvous at Grand Portage. The well protected cove just west of the point was also used by indigenous people and missionaries as a campsite in their frequent travels between Grand Portage and Fort William. Pointe Au Père, named after an early Jesuit priest supposedly murdered by the natives during the regime of French fur trade, is now known as McKellar Point just south of Cloud Bay.

Métis (offspring of marriages between voyageurs and Native American women) and Ojibway families went to Pointe Au Père and the other fishing stations each year to catch trout and whitefish for subsistence and the market. Each September, they paddled their fishing canoes and small bateaux to the remote fishing camps to catch and salt down as many barrels of fish as possible before returning to Fort William in late November or early December.

Hudson's Bay Company bateaux made frequent trips to the scattered fish camps bringing salt, barrels and other supplies and returning to Fort William with barrels filled with salt fish. Many barrels of salt fish would be consumed along with hundreds of bushels of potatoes – the winter diet of about 40 employees and about 200 First Nations people of the Fort William community. The 200 to 300 barrels of fish left over after winter consumption were shipped to Sault Ste. Marie via the schooner *Whitefish* each spring. From there, most of the fish were shipped through American companies east and south into the Ohio Valley.

Except for a few brief mentions in company diaries and Jesuit journals, very little has been recorded giving us greater details of the fishing methods and activities during the 1820s to 1870s. Questions of kinds and sizes of canoes, boats and schooners will have to be answered with educated guesses. The best we can do is borrow information gathered from other areas engaged in similar activities and apply them to Fort William. It's probable that Fort William fishermen used the same style bateaux, Mackinaw boats and canoes used at the Sault.

I hope that Pointe Au Père looked the same 150 years ago as it does now and that my interpretation of the fish camp and bateaux is close to being right.

Return of the War Party

The comings and goings of Native American war parties in the mid-1800s should be dramatic events worthy of extensive reporting by those witnessing the activity. Maybe it was, for other members of the tribe, who waved good-bye or shouted greetings from shore. But the Jesuit priests took such events nonchalantly in stride, with barely a mention in their writings, if Dominic du Ranquet's journal of 1856 is typical:

"… men from each band left in the Treaty of Mississippi for an expedition against the Sioux. These ones took some cannons."

"… Wabiskissinan and Katons arrive, a Sioux scalp at the head of the canoe."

These are the only mentions I have found of the continuing skirmishes between Grand Portage Ojibway and the Sioux. No further information or description. Just one or two lines sandwiched insignificantly between reporting of church doings in du Ranquet's journal.

Although chased by powerful Iroquois tribes from the Atlantic coast in the late 1500s, the Ojibway gained a reputation as fearless warriors after pushing the Sioux and Fox nations from Lake Superior shores in the 1600s and 1700s. After the Ojibway settled at La Pointe in the Apostle Islands, skirmishes between Sioux and Ojibway were regular events for more than 200 years.

Some Ojibway warriors fought on the French side during the French and Indian War in the mid-1700s. Some fought the British at Michilimacinac. The Ojibway remained neutral during the War of 1812.

There was no organized Ojibway army. No orderly chain of command. Individuals fought only when they chose to and quit anytime they desired, without being disciplined by a higher rank. A chief had to convince each warrior to join his cause.

In his narrative *30 Years of Captivity Among the Indians*, John Tanner described the events of an Ojibway war party against the Sioux in the late 1700s. A Muskegoe chief from lower Canada invited Assiniboin Cree and Ojibway warriors to march with his Muskegoe Band against his enemy, the Sioux. About 100 warriors marched hundreds of miles to the Sioux camp. But, along the way, warrior after warrior became disenchanted with the mission and returned home. By the time the dwindling army reached the Sioux camp, only five warriors remained. After a brief discussion of the situation they, too, returned home without shooting an arrow.

It seems that after the Ojibway beat the Sioux in the decisive Battle of the Falls on the St. Croix River in 1771, their skirmishes were more of a nuisance to each other than having lasting military importance.

As settlers started surging west, peace parties such as the Lewis Cass and Henry Schoolcraft expeditions tried to make peace between the Sioux and Ojibway to create a safe environment for trade and settlers. Several treaties in the mid-1800s finally put an end to major conflicts between warring tribes, transferred their lands to the United States and created reservations.

Except for a few scrapes now and then, hardly important enough to mention in Jesuit missionary journals, peace finally arrived in Lake Superior country.

Carrying the Priest Ashore at Dawson Bay – 1851

Father Frederic Baraga seems to have set the standards of what it took to be a successful Jesuit missionary to Lake Superior's tribal people and other inhabitants from the 1830s on. It was the snowshoe priest's tireless energy, indomitable spirit, fearless nature and genuine dedication to his beloved natives that made him an example to those priests who followed him into the wilderness. He was instrumental in establishing missions at Fond du Lac, Grand Portage and Fort William, in addition to his primary mission at La Pointe in the Apostle Islands.

Father Otto Skolla soon joined Baraga at La Pointe. By 1842, Father Franz Pierz established a mission at the mouth of the Pigeon River on the Canadian-Minnesota border. Father Pierre Choné joined Father Pierz at the Pigeon River and in 1849 helped him move that mission to Fort William. Fathers Nicolas Frémiot and Dominic Du Ranquet joined the mission soon after.

Like Father Baraga, these missionary priests traveled to their far-flung flocks by snowshoes, dog sleds, canoes, bateaux and Mackinaw boats in all seasons regardless of weather and hardships. Native Americans from Lake of the Woods, Lake Nipigon, Isle Royale and Grand Portage received religious instruction and the sacraments, baptisms and weddings from the hardy priests stationed at Fort William.

The painting "Piggyback Priest" tries to illustrate a typical trip to Isle Royale as recorded by Father Frémiot in 1851. He would, as the spirit moved him, roust out a couple of guides early in the morning, borrow a canoe or bateau and set sail for Isle Royale to serve the native fishermen and Irish copper miners working on the island.

If the weather turned bad along the way from Fort William, they stopped overnight in Dawson Bay on Pie Island at the mouth of Thunder Bay. The priest spent the night rolled up in a buffalo robe, while his guides slept under the boat. No matter when the wind subsided they continued across the open lake to Todd Harbor, many times rowing, paddling and sailing the 20 miles by moonlight.

The priests were famous for traveling in terrible weather conditions, not packing enough food, making the guides do all the hard work while they sat in the boat bottom reading scripture, praying and giving all the credit for a successful crossing to God. It may be the reason many local Native Americans were hard to find when the priests looked for guides.

Many of the guides were ex-voyageurs, whose tradition was to carry dignitaries ashore on their backs. The painting shows the priest being carried piggyback from the bateaux to the beach at Dawson Bay.

Dawson Bay was also a seasonal fishing camp of the Hudson's Bay Company at Fort William and one might find lodge poles, boat rollers and miscellaneous fishing paraphernalia left on the site year after year.

H. Siverson
©1999

Father du Ranquet and Company En Route to Mass at Grand Portage – 1852

During the mid-1800s, our frontier was rapidly moving west. The California Gold Rush was in full swing. Pioneers in wagon trains traveled the Oregon Trail, accompanied by Christian missionaries.

Meanwhile, on the western Lake Superior frontier, Jesuit priests from Fort William were busy making their rounds serving Native Americans and white people alike from Nipigon, Lake of the Woods, Grand Portage and Isle Royale. Although the fur trade was a mere shadow of its former self and Fort William had declined in importance as a fur trade post, it still remained an important supply depot for the district.

The majority of the French Canadian, Métis and Ojibway peoples of the Fort William community were Catholic, as were those at Grand Portage, Nipigon, Isle Royale and all the wilderness between. Irish Catholic miners at Isle Royale also felt a need for the church.

Journals by Father Nicolas Frémiot and Father Dominic du Ranquet describe their journeys to serve Catholics scattered about their district. Hair-raising trips in small boats across Lake Superior to Isle Royale and narrow escapes surviving winter treks on snowshoes are described in detail. Heroic and miraculous adventures sometimes rival those of Moses parting the Red Sea in the *Exodus*.

But many of their journeys were relatively uneventful and may even have been pleasurable. Certainly the scenery along the way was spectacularly beautiful as they coasted the shores between Fort William and Grand Portage.

I decided to paint Father du Ranquet with a party of worshippers on their way to Mass at Grand Portage from Fort William. If the priest was blessed, he may have been able to borrow a Mackinaw schooner-barge to sail lazily past escarpments like this one on Pine Point near Pigeon Bay. The Hudson's Bay Company at Fort William used various kinds of canoes, bateaux and barges for fishing and other fort business and on occasion lent craft like the Mackinaw schooner to their neighbors at the mission on the mouth of the Kaministiquia River.

A trip to Grand Portage could take two or three days, requiring the priest and entourage to camp overnight along the way.

Shore Lunch with Father du Ranquet – 1853

In 1849, Father Pierre Choné moved the church at the mouth of the Pigeon River to Mission Island at the mouth of the Kaministiquia River near Fort William. Two years later, Father Dominic du Ranquet constructed another church at Grand Portage to better serve Native American families and fur traders in that area.

This necessitated frequent trips between Fort William and Grand Portage in all seasons and all kinds of weather by the Jesuit priests. It was a two- to three-day journey each way that exposed the priests to drastic changes in weather along the voyage. Frostbite was common in winter, since priests and native guides were caught in blizzards and extreme cold while snowshoeing on inland trails or across the frozen lake. Sudden squalls and high winds threatened to swamp their small canoes and boats during seasons of travel on open waterways. Shifting ice packs in spring threatened to crush their frail craft, forcing them ashore to continue the trip afoot or wait for a shift in wind direction.

Under normal conditions, the trip by water required one or two overnight stays at scattered campsites along the way. Old camps, used through the years by Ojibway people, voyageurs,

fishermen, priests and mail carriers, provided shelter for travelers along the lake shore. Brule Point, Prince's Mine, Andokwaganing, Pointe Au Père, Tousleu Point and Pigeon Point were popular resting spots along the way.

I think it's possible that on some of those warm, beautiful days in July or August, with a gentle breeze blowing, the priests or other travelers might be tempted to vary their route slightly to explore new scenes and avoid monotony. To take a lunch break in the Albert Islands next to Victoria Island would not be out of the question.

There's a natural landing for a Mackinaw boat, a flat area to pull out canoes and a rock table for lunch. It would give the travelers a place to stretch their legs, the priest to offer a brief instruction in the faith and young warrior to hunt the wary sea gull with his favorite hunting dog.

From such a vantage point, the travelers could watch the horizon for the sails of schooners like the *Algonquin*, *Whitefish*, *Swallow*, *Uncle Tom* and *Fur Trader*. They may even be fortunate enough to see the new propeller steamers, *Baltimore*, *Independence* or *Napoleon* on their occasional trips to Fort William, Isle Royale and Grand Portage.

Immigrants Land at Beaver Bay – 1856

The first ship to pass through the new lock at Sault Ste. Marie in 1855 was also the ship that dropped off the first settlers at Beaver Bay a year later.

On June 24, 1856, the side-wheel steamer, *Illinois*, eased its bow onto the sand beach just east of the mouth of the Beaver River, where it unloaded the Weiland family and several other Swiss and German settlers from the Maumee Valley of Ohio. Twenty-three men, women and children along with horses, cows, oxen, pigs, chickens, household goods, wagons and farm tools were put ashore on the edge of Lake Superior's north shore wilderness to shift for themselves.

They shifted well indeed. Within six weeks of wading ashore, the little colony had built seven houses, two shanties, cleared 12 acres, four of which they got into crops, made seven miles of wagon road and cut 12 tons of wild hay. They raised wheat and later built a grist mill to provide flour and feed.

Wood, harvested from extensive stands of white pine, was used to build their small settlement and in 1869 the Weiland brothers built a water-powered sawmill at the Beaver River mouth to saw lumber for export to other communities along the shore.

The first load of lumber was hauled by Captain Asa Parker aboard his schooner, *George W. Ford*, to his home at Ontonagon.

After that, the Weiland brothers bought the schooner *Charley* that delivered their lumber to Marquette, Ontonagon, Copper Harbor, Eagle River, Duluth and Prince Arthur's Landing in Thunder Bay.

The Weilands were among the first white settlers to take advantage of the Fond du Lac Treaty with the Lake Superior Band of Ojibway in 1856 that opened the north shore to settlement. The earlier Treaty of La Pointe in 1854 allowed for mineral speculation only. Prospectors, looking for copper, silver and iron ore, were among the first wave of immigrants to surge onto Lake Superior's north shore. Finding no minerals of consequence, most moved on. But others settled to make their subsistence by logging, commercial fishing, trapping and some farming.

Ships like the *Illinois* hustled through the Soo Locks after 1855 to serve the growing settlements and new industries around the lake. The first fatal collision between ships in Lake Superior came on August 9, 1862. The steamer *Illinois*, eastbound in thick fog on a dark night off Munising with a load of iron ore from Marquette, literally cut the 141-foot schooner *Oriole* in two, killing 10 crewmen and two passengers. *Illinois* survived with little damage, only to be sunk at Eagle River in 1864 by a violent June storm. It was raised again and smoke from its stacks continued to mark its rounds of Lake Superior ports for years after.

Boat Day at Parkerville

In 1874, the travel guide *Sailing on the Great Lakes* described Parkerville as "a small settlement situated at the mouth of the Pigeon River, where also is to be seen Indian huts and wigwams constructed of birch bark. This place, no doubt, is soon destined to become a place of resort during the summer months. It is situated about 130 miles northeast of Duluth."

But instead of fulfilling that destiny, Parkerville was abandoned in 1877 and, instead of becoming a place of resort, the small settlement returned to wilderness. If you have never heard of Parkerville, you are not alone. Very few people have and facts are hard to come by.

The site of Parkerville is about halfway between the High Falls and mouth of the Pigeon River and had a small fur-trading post from 1795 to 1804, when it was abandoned and moved to Fort William along with the rest of the North West Company interests.

Jesuit Father Franz Pierz started to build a birch chapel near the site in 1842 but was transferred to another mission before it was completed. Father Otto Skolla reported that the mission chapel was still without a roof four years later. Other priests reopened the mission in 1848, then abandoned it shortly thereafter to build a mission near the Hudson's Bay Company at Fort William.

Asa Aldis Parker, the founder of Parkerville, first arrived at Pigeon River as a surveyor in 1859 and found the area so favorable that he acquired 1,472 acres. He moved his family from Ontonagon in 1867 to prospect for minerals, trade furs and fish commercially. He also raised wheat, potatoes, vegetables, cattle, hogs, chickens, flowers and fruit trees.

Asa, wife, Caroline, and three children were soon joined by the Sam Howenstein family and several other settlers, including William Farr, William Steich, Charles Anderson, Charles Parker, Daniel Parker and William Parker, relatives of Asa. A total population of 16 lived in three houses.

Parkerville became a post office in about 1866, handling mail from Duluth and Port Arthur. The schooner *Charley* carried the mail in summer, while dog teams made deliveries during freeze-up. The post office at Parkerville closed in 1877, just two years after Asa Parker left Parkerville and returned to Ontonagon.

The painting "Boat Day at Parkerville" shows the supply boat *George W. Ford*, owned and operated by Captain John Parker, arriving with supplies. *George W. Ford* was one of the first schooners to be towed across the portage at Sault Ste. Marie before the locks were built in 1855. Asa's brother John used the schooner *Ford* to haul supplies to Asa and other settlers on Lake Superior and to return to his Ontonagon store with furs and fish. The schooner was wrecked at Eagle Harbor on August 20, 1870.

The settlement of Parkerville lasted for only 10 years. The panic of 1873, the coming of the Canadian railroad, the sinking of the schooner *Ford*, the Howensteins returning to Grand Marais, the Parkers returning to Ontonagon and the arresting of the deputy postmaster C.K. Jackson – an accessory to a murder – all claimed its toll on one of the smallest, most short-lived, but interesting settlements on the north shore.

H. Siverson
©1999

T.H. Camp Picking up Fish – 1876

Commercial fishing on the United States side of Lake Superior subsided drastically after the demise of the American Fur Company in 1842. Fish production lay almost dormant for a decade, with a few exceptions, after Ramsay Crooks took the last of his fishing fleet to Detroit. The Hudson's Bay Company at Fort William continued to catch fish for export. Ojibway and Métis people immigrated each summer to Isle Royale to harvest fish for their own use and to sell to copper miners at Rock Harbor. Hugh McCullough, owner of the Grand Portage trading post, moved his fishermen into the abandoned American Fur Company fish camps around Isle Royale to catch fish for export. But most of the fishing activity on Lake Superior continued to be on the south shore where Native Americans and ex-employees of the American Fur Company continued to survive by fishing during the lean 1840s.

After the Civil War, commercial fishing once again grew to be an important industry. French and Native American fishermen were joined by an increasing flow of Scandinavian immigrants, who brought new fishing technology from the old country. Although most U.S. fishing was concentrated around growing settlements like Bayfield, Ashland and Duluth, many fishermen scattered themselves along the north and south shores at isolated fishing camps. Many of those fishermen were grubstaked by large fish companies like the A. Booth Company that supplied or sold the equipment and supplies needed and paid for by fish caught. To service those scattered fish camps, the A. Booth Company put on their first steam-powered tug, *T.H. Camp*, and tried to make regularly scheduled runs about the western end of Lake Superior and Isle Royale.

From its home base in Bayfield, the *Camp* made frequent trips to deliver mail, groceries, supplies, salt, barrels and passengers to fish stations as far away as the Ontario-Minnesota border from 1876 to 1900. The painting shows how it may have looked picking up fish at Little Indian Cove near Pigeon Bay.

In 1888, just two years before the *Camp* sank in the Apostle Islands, the Booth Company added the larger *Hiram Dixon* to assist the *T.H. Camp*. In 1902, *Dixon* was replaced by the Booth Company's last ship, the steamer *America* that served western Lake Superior until 1928, when it sank at Isle Royale.

Stranger Goes Missing – December 12, 1875

For some unknown reason, Captain Isaac Clark sailed his little 60-foot schooner *Stranger* up the treacherous north shore of Lake Superior in the most dangerous season of the year without his anchor. He was in such a hurry to reach Grand Marais that he even refused the offer by Alfred Merritt to use the anchor from his schooner *Handy*. Captain Clark probably figured that the harbor at Grand Marais would offer protection at that time of year. It was the little freighter's last trip of the season, loaded with supplies the small isolated community at Grand Marais needed to survive the winter. The sooner he left Duluth, the sooner he'd return. To leave without an anchor aboard proved, however, to be a fatal mistake.

With a southwest wind pushing it along, the *Stranger* arrived at Grand Marais at 2 p.m., December 12, 1875, to find the growing seas too heavy in the west bay to unload its cargo. High winds, now coming from the northwest, along with freezing temperatures complicated conditions that required Captain Clark to turn once again into the open lake in an attempt to round the point to gain more protection in the east bay. With rigging and tackle frozen solid by the subzero temperature, the *Stranger* failed to manage the turn into the east bay and crashed against the shallow reef extending from the point. Unable to come about into the wind and with no anchor to hold its position, *Stranger* drifted helplessly out to sea, its hold rapidly filling with water.

Crewman George Coburn was swept overboard and drowned as the schooner turned on its side in heavy seas. Joe Cadotte and Jimmy La Fave desperately chopped down its two masts and frozen rigging and the *Stranger* righted itself again.

On shore, witnesses to its plight formed a rescue party and launched a small boat in an attempt to save the crew. Grand Marais citizens Jack Scott, John Morrison, Sam and son William Howenstein made a heroic effort, reaching the helpless schooner and managing to throw lines aboard. But the ship's crew was too weakened and frozen to catch the lines and boarding it was out of the question.

The rescue boat crew was soon exhausted and needed their remaining strength to save themselves. The *Stranger* and frozen crew drifted off, sinking in the raging storm – never to be heard of or seen again.

The rescuers survived, after reaching shore 30 miles east of Grand Marais.

Walking the Plank – 1888

The "Copper Rush" on Lake Superior began before the "Gold Rush" in California. Mineral prospectors swarmed over the lake's shores throughout the 19th century, but serious mining didn't start until the 1840s. Copper and iron mining companies established communities on Isle Royale and along the south shore requiring freight, passenger and mail service provided by early sailing and steam propeller ships. Logging companies and commercial fishermen also needed lake transportation to service their growing industries.

The need for regularly scheduled boat service along the north shore, caused by the increasing flow of immigrants, growing numbers of commercial fishermen and demands of a burgeoning tourist industry, was met by the A. Booth Company steamship *Hiram Dixon* in 1888. Regularly scheduled trips, two per week, were welcomed by members of isolated communities scattered along the shore and Isle Royale. No longer would they have to spend day after day scanning the horizon for sporadic trips by the old *T.H. Camp*.

In August 1888, the *Dixon* started running two round trips per week from Duluth to Port Arthur and Isle Royale, carrying everything imaginable except the mail. John Beargrease continued delivering the mail via rowboat and dog sled for two more years.

Because there were no roads along the north shore until the 1920s, everything that the early settlers needed had to come on boats by water. Orders – verbal and written – for groceries, clothes, hardware, lumber, furniture, farming, fishing, lumbering and mining equipment and supplies were shouted or handed over the railing to the captain from the men in fragile skiffs bobbing in the seas next to the ship.

No one aboard was surprised when the list included farm animals. On the next trip of the *Dixon,* the menagerie would be delivered. Chickens, pigs and goats were unloaded directly into skiffs, but horses and cows were forced to walk the plank extending through the side hatch and suspended over the water. Once prodded to the water end of the plank, the other end was lifted, launching the animal into the frigid lake. It didn't take long for horse or cow to swim to the nearest shore, guided by the happy owner in a skiff.

Hiram Dixon continued in service until 1902, when the Booth Company replaced it with the faster, sleeker, more luxurious steamship *America*.

Trip to Town

Travel along the north shore in the 1800s was by foot in winter and by boat in summer. Sometimes it took both to get to your destination. Prior to the automobile, people were accustomed to walking long distances. Walking from Duluth to Pigeon River on frozen Lake Superior would have been considered normal in the late 1800s.

So, in the spring of 1899, when Ed Tofte from Tofte and Charlie Johnson and George Mayhew from Grand Marais grew impatient waiting for the first trip of the steamer *Hiram Dixon* to take them home, no one was surprised when they decided to walk. They left Two Harbors in March carrying long spruce poles to prevent their sinking through holes in the ice should they crash through, which they did several times before reaching Beaver Bay. Lake Superior's ice fields are in constant motion, breaking up, moving about and freezing again. Some sections comprised of old ice could be 4 inches to 36 inches thick. Some sections of new ice, formed between old sections that drift together at odd angles, may only be a half-inch thick. After a snowfall covers the ice, it all looks the same.

They encountered large areas of open water outside of Beaver Bay, where they managed to rent a rowboat from a local fisherman. They rowed the boat to the next ice field, pulled and pushed the rowboat over the ice until encountering the next open water, then repeated the process until reaching their destination. A trip like that today would be considered foolhardy and unthinkable, but it was just another trip to town for north shore pioneers.

Until recent times, walking long distances was common. Settlers walked from Missouri to California. Soldiers walked home from the Civil War. Early pioneers walked from St. Paul to Duluth carrying nothing but a blanket and a loaf of bread. Explorers from fur trade companies walked across Canada and back again. Native people traveled afoot across the length and breadth of North America carrying all their belongings with them.

Much of long distance traveling was done in winter when waterways were frozen and snowshoe trails were packed down. Falling through thin ice, frostbite and frozen limbs, deadly cold and blizzards, starvation and injuries were common hazards of the journey. But, on the brighter side, there were no congested freeways or time clocks to punch.

H. Sivertson
© 2001

A Goat in a Boat Full Of Oats

Immigrants from Norway began to arrive in Tofte in the late 1800s and early 1900s. They fished, farmed and logged to survive in the little settlement along the north shore.

In the spring of 1906, Hans Engleson was getting desperate for oats to feed the draft horses used in his logging operation near Tofte. The only oats available were at the Lutsen logging camp about nine miles to the northeast. Because there were no roads along the shore in those days, the oats would have to be fetched by water. But the lake's shifting frozen ice packs were pushed hard against the shore, making boat travel impossible. Finally, in March, an offshore wind drove the ice away from shore, leaving a channel of water wide enough to chance a voyage to Lutsen and the precious oats.

Matt Johnson, Ole Norwick and Mons Monson boarded Matt's Mackinaw fishing schooner for the rescue mission to Lutsen. They arrived at the logging camp safely, taking advantage of the northwest breeze. After loading the boat to the gunwales with sacks of oats, they were about to depart for Tofte when someone remembered that Hans Engleson's billy goat had wintered at the Lutsen logging camp and Hans wanted him back. This was a good opportunity to return the goat, so the billy was loaded aboard and they set sail for Tofte.

Meanwhile, the wind had shifted to the southeast, driving the massive ice field back toward the north shore. The race was on. Relentlessly the ice moved toward the fragile craft threatening to crush it against the shore. Heavily loaded, the boat rode low in the water, giving the ice a solid target to push against.

Unloading the oats let the boat rise in the water, giving the onrushing ice less of a target and making it possible for the men to maneuver the little Mackinaw out of harm's way.

Again the wind shifted, blowing the ice field with the discarded sacks of oats out to sea. Again the schooner returned to Lutsen for another load of oats and this time returned safely – goat, boat, oats and all – back to Tofte and the hungry horses.

America at Tofte Dock

A typical trip on the steamer *America* in the early 1900s was an unforgettable experience for most passengers. Captain "Indian" Smith steered the sleek Booth Company ship through the piers at Duluth for another two-day excursion along the north shore to Port Arthur, Isle Royale and back. One anonymous passenger described his unforgettable trip:

"We sat on the afterdeck, watching the Duluth Harbor fade away behind its industrial curtain of smoke as we head for Two Harbors, our first port of call, 20 miles up the shore. We ran in behind the breakwater and tied up at a little dock in the shadow of the giant ore docks that dominate the harbor. Presently the banging of the freight on the dock ceased, the *America* tooted her whistle, the engine bell rang to back her and she turned around, stuck her prow out through the channel under the lighthouse and we entered the open lake again.

"The *America* runs so close to shore that the eternal black rocks and dark red cliffs may be plainly seen; the former fringed with the dashing white of breaking surf and the latter crowned with the waving green of northland foliage. Far back from shore the granite hills of Sawtooth Range rise to varying heights of several hundred feet with lines of higher altitude farther inland. Unexpected little bays and valleys are revealed as the steamer rounds one point after another.

"In each of these curving harbors are the dwellings of fisher folk, their log homes being far enough back to escape the surf, while close to the jagged black shoreline are tiny shelters where fish are packed and salted. Alongside of these will be seen boats drawn up on pole skidways and reels for drying nets, while in front little docks jut out for making difficult landings.

"The next port on our schedule is Beaver Bay, where we see a double-pointed boat making out from shore, its oarsman standing up facing the bow and rowing so skillfully in this unusual fashion that the great rollers, though they stand his little craft fairly on end, are conquered safely and he places himself, apparently, right where our high prow will smash his skiff to pieces. But the brown-armed Norseman cunningly guides his leaping rolling little craft and is right alongside. A rope is thrown to him, he seizes it, draws his boat up under the gunwale of the steamer, which has come to a stop, and the difficult business of unloading freight from a drifting steamer into a leaping skiff begins and is carried to a happy conclusion with a case of beer. The sturdy oarsman signs a bill of lading, casts off the rope, waves farewell and guides his heavily loaded skiff towards the surf-beaten rocks in the distance."

The unknown author continues to describe the loading and unloading of passengers along the route, who agilely leap from skiff to ship, timing their jumps perfectly in rhythm with the tossing seas. He poetically describes sitting on deck at night watching moonlight dancing on the water.

His fellow passengers include ladies in all their finery, businessmen, lumberjacks and commercial fishermen who, side by side, play slot machines in the palatial saloon under crystal chandeliers. Meals are served in a first class, ornate dining room to the accompaniment of live organ music.

After rendezvousing with about 400 fishermen along the shore and Isle Royale, *America* returns to Duluth, stopping at the newly built concrete dock jutting out into the open lake at Tofte. The trip was truly memorable even if some fog was encountered or if *America* was caught up in one of Lake Superior's famous storms – in which case the trip would be absolutely unforgettable.

Homeward

The days and nights of commercial fishermen along the north shore were often cold and lonely. Before dawn each morning, from April to fall freeze-up, fishermen pushed their 18-foot wooden skiffs off the slides next to their fish houses perched on rocks in sheltered coves, to attend their nets offshore. Early morning, before the wind picked up, was the best time for working on the lake.

In spring the lake was about the same temperature as ice. In summer the surface water temperature climbed to 55 degrees to 60 degrees for a short time in August. Then early fall storms with heavy seas turned the lake water over, mixing surface water with deep water. The lake cooled rapidly until, by mid-February, it froze. For just a few days in summer, the fishermen could work on the lake without a heavy jacket and long underwear.

The rest of the year, long wool underwear, wool shirts, wool socks and heavy duty rubber clothes kept the men from freezing. Cold weather and cold water toughened the fishermen to the point that they could pick herring nets in subzero temperatures with their bare hands. When hands started to freeze, they merely stuck them in the lake for a few minutes to thaw out. The lake temperature, being a balmy 32.5 degrees above zero, was warm by comparison to the much colder air.

North shore fishermen have been caught out on the lake by sudden storms, blizzards, high winds and extremely cold temperatures that froze hands to oars and boots to skiff bottoms. Some didn't survive.

Fishermen's homesteads were scattered miles apart in the early years, making social contact a rare event. Those who were married with children had their families for companionship. Bachelor fishermen's lives were lonelier, although some preferred it that way.

The painting "Homeward" was inspired by my experiences commercial fishing at Isle Royale as a youth on summer vacations from school. Even in summer, I looked forward to returning home from the cold lake winds to the warm, sheltered harbor and a hot cup of coffee around a cozy wood stove with friends.

Squall Over Grandpa Sam's Fish House

Grover Cleveland was elected president of the United States the same year – 1892 – that Sam and Theodora Sivertson arrived from Norway and built their first fish house at Washington Harbor, Isle Royale. It was the decade of the Spanish-American War, the Klondike Gold Rush, the shooting of Sitting Bull and the Battle of Wounded Knee. The Oklahoma land rush in 1893 symbolized that American pioneers were moving west. Utah became a state, Buffalo Bill's Wild West Shows were all the rage and radios and automobiles hadn't been invented yet.

There are more than 200 islands that make up the archipelago of Isle Royale. Sam picked the wrong one on which to build his first fish house. The owner of the island, John Johns, tore the fish house down that winter and Sam found it stacked neatly at the end of the dock the next spring with orders, in English – which Sam didn't understand – to take his fish house elsewhere.

Somehow, Sam understood the message and moved his shack across the bay to Singer Island on the property that he had purchased next to the new Singer tourist hotel. But unsightly, smelly fish houses create the wrong ambiance for the posh tourist trade and Singer bought Grandpa's property. He then moved his operation farther down the bay, out of sight and smell of the hotel.

Sam's new fish house was built on a dock made of rock-filled log cribs, typical of fish house construction in harbors protected from wind, seas and ice movement. My painting shows the fish house as it looked 60 years after it was built. The rowboat and skiff on the boat slide looked about the same as they did when Sam arrived. The "Gas Boat" at the dock evolved from Mackinaw sailing schooners that Grandpa first used upon his arrival at the island. The recently invented gasoline engines were soon adapted to power the old Mackinaw schooners and, after several decades, the masts and sails disappeared as confidence in machines grew.

Besides the obvious use as a place to process fish and store fishing paraphernalia, the fish house was a gathering place where other fishermen and island folks stopped by to see the day's catch, to help in the processing and to spin yarns. It was great entertainment for us kids to listen to the drama of the day's adventures on the wild, mysterious lake. We picked up a few neat words to use on special occasions, also. Words that if heard by the wrong people could get your mouth washed out with soap.

There were also a few minutes after the fish were dressed, iced down in boxes or salted down in kegs that folks sat on gas barrels, fish boxes or kegs and continued the yarns, until the dinner bell rang and dispersed the group.

Gust

Gust never planned a day in his life. Other people planned Gust's life for him. He was called a bum by some. A happy-go-lucky, ne'er-do-well who may or may not have been a product of the era he grew up in. He got hooked on alcohol during Prohibition and looked for work during the Depression. But work was scarce and easy to avoid in the 1930s when Gust and his cronies lived in hobo camps and rode the rods across country ostensibly looking for work. Gust told me that he never had so much fun, but you had to watch your back. He, like some other men of his ilk, followed the harvest seasons of wheat, logs and fish and could be well-heeled one day and broke the next. Wine, women and song.

Wine and song were Gust's specialties. He loved them both. If it weren't for wine, you'd know Gust as the great Swedish tenor Gustave Bjorlin from the Met. He loved opera, trained himself, knew all the words and sang beautifully and loud after just a few drinks.

Gust was a good worker, once caught, cleaned and sobered up. The man-catchers from the logging camps caught Gust each fall to work in the woods. He was great with horses, which I think he loved more than he loved people. Sometimes the work farm caught him. Police were alerted to watch for Gust and when he got drunk and disorderly (singing too loud), he was shipped to the work farm. He was a wonderful and good-natured cook and they looked forward to his presence whenever he could be caught.

About the first of April each year, my dad combed the bowery in Duluth to catch him for another season of commercial fishing at Isle Royale. He wasn't hard to find. Dad drove his car with the window down through the three-block-long bowery district until he homed in on Gust's gorgeous arias. Gust was always in good humor, especially when tipsy, and was easily caught, lured with a bottle of whisky to board the boat to Isle Royale.

In his shack at Isle Royale, Dad scrubbed him down, deloused him, dressed him in clean clothes, removed all the sharp objects from the room, closed the door, locked it from the outside and left Gust alone to fight his snakes.

In two days, he was let out to face a terrible hangover and the brilliant sun that overexposed his already white, pasty face. He stumbled over rocks and roots down the path to the fish house, where a quart of buttermilk waited for him in the ice box. Gust chug-a-lugged the entire contents, some running down his chin onto his clean shirt, but most cooling his parched throat and brain and settling his stomach. He leaned against the fish dressing bench until the milk took effect, pulled on his rubber boots and rubber pants and walked unsteadily across the dock to the boat, where his partner Charlie Parker waited patiently at the tiller.

For years, Gust was the engineer of the converted Buick gasoline engine that seemed to be waiting for his knowing touch. After fumbling about the controls that he knew so well, Gust finally got the engine started. He straightened up, put hands on hips, turned to Charlie and smiled his first smile of the new season.

"Welcome home," shouted Charlie over the engine noise, standing on the stern seat with tiller between his knees ready to cast off the lines.

In a few days, hard work in sun and fresh air on the open lake and Grandma's home cooking, Uncle Gust's muscles firmed up and his skin took on a ruddy glow. He was ready for nine months of commercial fishing and mandatory sobriety on Isle Royale, where whisky was scarce.

He and Charlie would fish hooklines for lake trout in a boat similar to the one in the painting, then net fish until November, when he'd be paid off. After a few days of fighting temptation on the mainland, he'd meander to the bowery until he heard his cronies call, "Hey, Gust," from behind the saloon doors. You know the rest of the story.

Isle Royale Moose Mystery

When you think of Isle Royale, it's difficult not to think of moose and wolves, the island's most recognized symbols and subjects of intensive scientific study for the last half century. Yet, neither of the species is indigenous to the island and both are recent immigrants to its shores. Moose mysteriously appeared around 1904-05. Wolves followed about 45 years later. There are several theories on how they arrived, but no proof is anywhere in sight.

Isle Royale is a 210-square-mile archipelago in Lake Superior, 15 to 20 miles off Ontario's shores, the closest mainland. Once in a great while an extremely cold winter will create an ice cover over the entire lake that could last from mid-February to mid-March. Moose are not herding animals like caribou and are not fond of traveling on ice, so what force in nature would entice them to make the long trip to Isle Royale on the ice pack?

The theory that moose migrated to Isle Royale on ice is highly questionable. Why would moose head for a land mass they couldn't see or smell on treacherous ice they usually try to avoid? Cow moose may lure a bull to do extraordinary feats, but by February she'd have lost those charms. If wolves chased moose out on the ice, why didn't they follow them all the way to the island? In order for the moose on Isle Royale to explode to 3,000 animals in 30 years, many bulls and cows would have had to make the senseless journey during the short period of time when the rarely occurring ice bridge was intact.

Another similar theory is that moose swam to the island from Canada. Here, again, the same questions should be asked. What would lure them or force them to swim 15 to 20 miles across Lake Superior's choppy seas to an island they can't see, hear or smell?

Bobby Don Brazell, a logger and lifetime resident of Grand Marais, Minnesota, vaguely recalls a story about his father or grandfather, who claimed to have hauled live moose to Isle Royale in his fish tug. Even though Bobby didn't know why or when, the story lends credence to the most plausible theory yet.

Through a reliable grapevine, Bill Peterson from the Minnesota Department of Natural Resources in Grand Marais learned from an old-timer in Baudette that he was a member of a crew hired by Michigan about 1905-1906 to live-trap moose to be sent to Isle Royale for an unknown purpose. They captured 11 or 13 moose, hauled them to Two Harbors and loaded them on barges for Isle Royale. Records of the event were lost by the Conservation Department or burned when the Two Harbors newspaper building caught on fire.

Lending credence to that story, a recent genetic study shows that the Isle Royale moose herd is directly related to the Baudette herd. But why they were captured, crated and hauled to Isle Royale remains a mystery. Who benefited? Who paid the expenses?

After hearing the Baudette theory, an Isle Royale historian speculated that a sportsmen's club at Washington Harbor ordered the moose. A group of well-to-do sportsmen from downstate Minnesota took over the abandoned mine building in Washington Harbor and started the "Washington Club" in the late 1800s. They needed a new species of animal to hunt when caribou became scarce. The moose from Baudette were transplanted to Isle Royale for that purpose. Maybe Bobby Don's grandfather's moose were for the same purpose. We'll probably never know.

If the Baudette theory is true, we must conclude that the sportsmen were lousy shots for the moose herd to grow from a few stragglers in 1905 to more than 3,000 animals by 1928.

Pete, Pals and Rock Harbor Light

Pete Edisen's island home was just a few hundred feet around the point from the Rock Harbor Lighthouse. Although Pete wasn't the most productive fisherman on Isle Royale, he is probably the most famous. His love for people, animals and storytelling are undoubtedly the reasons for his widespread fame. His friends the moose, beavers, foxes, squirrels, otters, eagles and sea gulls would come for a treat whenever Pete called.

Many are the stories of Pete, feeding his pals, the sea gulls, who would fight for the privilege of sitting on his head. It was common to see Pete cruising down the harbor in his skiff with a gull perched, balancing on his hat. He was frequently asked how he felt toward the gulls when they messed down the back of his neck. Pete's answer was, "If you want good friends, you have to take some crap."

Pete came to Isle Royale from Norway and in 1916 started commercial fishing near Middle Island Passage in Rock Harbor. Soon after, he married fisherman Mike Johnson's daughter, Laura, and they spent the rest of their lives at the Edisen Fishery, where the coffee pot was always on and Pete's colorful stories kept visitors enthralled for hours.

Mike Johnson had two sons, too. Milford and Arnold married Myrtle and Olga and continued the family fishing tradition, taking up residence in the abandoned Rock Harbor Lighthouse during the early 1930s. One year, Milford's and Arnold's families wintered over on the island in total isolation from the outside world. Myrtle was pregnant when the last mail and passenger boat left the island in the fall, leaving her all winter to worry whether the first boat would arrive in the spring in time to take her to the mainland to have her baby. It did.

Rock Harbor Lighthouse was built in 1855 to guide the increasing number of ships that serviced the copper mines at Isle Royale. By the time it was completed the mines failed and, after four years, the light was turned off. It was rekindled again in 1874 during the second attempt to mine copper on the island, which lasted only five years. The light was extinguished for good in 1879 and then served as housing for fishing families.

Rock Harbor Lighthouse and Pete Edisen's Fishery are now on the rolls of the National Register of Historic Places and the fishery is an interpretation center for the Isle Royale National Park Service.

Rendezvous Off Shore – 1930s

Loading and unloading freight, passengers and mail at sea was tricky business off Isle Royale's rugged shore. Fishermen from small coves like Fisherman's Home, Hay Bay, Wright Island and Long Point had to load and unload offshore on ships like the *Winyah* that were too large to enter the small coves and bays that were home to their isolated fisheries. Passengers had to pick the right instant to leap from the ship's open hatch to the small skiff bobbing and heaving on heavy seas alongside. Loading the 100-pound boxes and kegs of fish onto the ship had to be timed perfectly or they were lost over the side. Mail and orders for groceries, clothes, equipment and supplies were exchanged, quickly, at the right moment. It was a common scene after the 1870s, aboard the *T.H. Camp, Hiram Dixon, America, Winyah* and finally the *Detroit* or "Pickle Boat" in the mid-1900s.

H. Christiansen and Sons Fishery in Duluth bought the 119.5-foot *Winyah* in 1924 and started running it along the north shore and Isle Royale after the Booth Company steamship *America* sank at Isle Royale in 1928. The original sleek, graceful yacht was built in 1894 for the wife of Andrew Carnegie, who named it the *Dungeness*. H. Christiansen remodeled it for freight service on Lake Superior and renamed it the *Winyah*. The company added another deck and stuck a pilothouse and staterooms on top of that, transforming the once gracious yacht into a top-heavy, roly-poly, ungainly looking freight boat.

After the road was built along the north shore in the 1920s, freight trucks started replacing freight boats to serve residents. Although shipping by water was phasing out from Duluth to Grand Portage, residents on Isle Royale still needed service by the *Winyah*.

Captains Martin Christiansen, Ole Berg and then Matt Hanson guided the *Winyah* around Isle Royale and along the north shore, without mishap, rarely missing a trip, until it retired from service in 1943. The loud, distinctive horn announced its arrival, usually right on schedule. Fishermen's boats filled with fish and family emerged from homes tucked in along the wild and rugged shoreline to rendezvous with *Winyah*, their only connection with the outside world.

H. Siverlson ©1999

Back to School

From early in the spring, when Dad started assembling his gear for Isle Royale in the hallway of our house in Duluth, I looked forward with great anticipation to my trip to the island in June. One night in mid-April we'd get a kiss on the cheek, his boxes disappeared from the hallway and Dad was gone to start another season of commercial fishing. Mother would join him in May and my sister and I would follow in June after school was out.

We stayed with various relatives until it was time to board the bus or a fish truck for the long gear-grinding trip to Grand Marais to board the steamer *Winyah* for another seasick adventure across to Isle Royale.

Dad and Mother met us at Booth Dock in Washington Harbor in the middle of the night. We followed Dad's flashlight to our boat for the short ride to our dock at the end of the harbor, then walked the long gravel path to our cabin with a lantern in the window. Then to my bed with quilts piled so high they pinned me to the horsehair mattress. The next day I awoke to another summer of island adventures with cousins and friends, seven in all, who would chase moose, squirrels, beaver, toads, frogs and fish. We'd swim, play hide-and-seek, go to island dances, sanger fests (song fests), picnics on the beach, speckle trout fishing, rowing regattas, poker games and berry picking. The thought of going back to school was a long way off, until the birch trees showed a tinge of yellow and the fishermen readied nets for fall fishing and moose antlers were losing their velvet.

It was time to place our orders for school clothes from the Sears and Roebuck or "Monkey" Wards catalogs. By the time the orders arrived there were just a few days left before we once more boarded the boats to take us back to school.

On the day of departure we bathed and put on our brand new, spanking clean, crisply pressed school clothes. I walked about stiff legged so I wouldn't bend the crease in my pants, careful not to touch anything that would soil my royal outfit. No wrestling in the grass, wading in the water, lying on my stomach fishing through holes in the fish house floor. Don't get near the gas barrels. The powdery red paint could jump on your new outfit from 3 feet away. The dress bench, fish boxes, cork rack, net reels, buoy rack, herring skiff and almost everything were out of bounds.

The queasy feeling began as we gathered on the dock, ready to leave, hugging friends and relatives for the last time this year. The fish boat had been washed down, clean fish boxes turned upside down for boat seats. The engine roared into action. Lines were untied and we backed away from the dock. We waved at the folks left behind until they were out of sight, then the long trip across the lake to Grand Portage began. The usual cloudy threatening day with southwest seas added to the depression I felt as I anticipated another $2\frac{1}{2}$-hour trip – and the strong probability of getting seasick and messing up my new clothes.

Some of the passengers huddled under blankets in the bow. Some, with stronger stomachs, were in high spirits anxious to meet winter friends again. Some of us just sat staring at the excruciatingly slow advancement of the distant strip of land on the horizon, wondering how long it would take before I fed the sea gulls my breakfast.

Herring Tug

The fall herring run out of Duluth was a spectacular fish harvesting event, comparable to fur trade rendezvous days, but with twice the work and half the fun. Every fall during the 1930s and '40s, it seemed like all the herring in Lake Superior gathered on the shallow banks in the southwest tip of the lake to spawn. Herring tugs from Two Harbors, Knife River, Herbster, Port Wing, Cornucopia and Bayfield came to Duluth to harvest the 10- to 12-inch silvery fish from November to January. Herring tugs crowded the docks in Duluth's harbor, as fishermen and fish processors worked around the clock catching, preparing and shipping hundreds of tons of herring to market around the country.

Tugs like the one in the painting left the harbor before dawn for the fishing grounds five to 10 miles from the harbor. They returned each night after dark looking like ice-encrusted coffins. Subzero temperatures caused frost smoke (frozen ice crystals) to rise hundreds of feet in the air and, along with spray from heavy fall seas, coated the 36-foot hulls with several inches of ice, giving the impression that everyone inside must be half frozen.

But it was actually hot inside the cabins, where the crew of four to six men was dressed in heavy wool clothes and rubber suits. Heat from the engine and coal stove at times became unbearable and hatches had to be opened to let cold air in to preserve the fish.

A gas-powered net lifter, mounted by the bow hatch, pulled nets full of herring into the boat and onto a long picking board that extended over the engine box to the stern of the boat, where one man gathered the net into boxes and prepared it for resetting. One fisherman stationed himself next to the lifter, guiding the net to several "pickers" stationed on each side of the picking table. The pickers untangled herring from the mesh and threw them into iced-down boxes. Sometimes there were too many fish for the men to handle and they were left in the nets to be picked out at night on land.

Once ashore, the fishermen gathered at the Metropole Hotel and Bar or People's Tavern, where they had rooms for the season, had a few drinks and supper. Some returned to the tugs for a long night of picking. Some continued celebrating the catch. All of them survived with just a few hours of sleep each night.

The annual fall herring run came to an end in the 1950s, when taconite tailings from the taconite plant in Silver Bay drifted to Duluth, covering the spawning grounds with silt and making the water too contaminated for herring to survive.

Trout For Food Or Fun

Commercial fishermen setting trout nets on McCormick Reef in September was a common scene on Isle Royale for more than 100 years. Boat design changed somewhat over the years since the American Fur Company started commercial fishing on the island in the 1830s, but basically it looked the same then as it did in the late 1940s as shown in the painting.

Annual fish harvests varied little during that 100 years, leaving the impression that the resource was unlimited. So as not to deplete the resource, commercial fishermen collected spawn and milt from lake trout caught before spawning season, resulting in a generous restocking program each year by the Conservation Department. Then, all of a sudden, trout began to disappear at a rapid rate.

Some experts accused commercial fishermen of overfishing, which in a sense they did. Anytime you kill one of a species already in decline, you have killed one too many. The real reason for the rapid decline in trout population, however, was due to the influx of a small voracious predator fish called smelt from Lake Michigan. Smelt invaded Lake Superior in the late 1940s and gorged themselves on trout spawn and fingerlings. Another predator, the sea lamprey, entered Lake Superior via the newly constructed St. Lawrence Seaway and attacked all mature trout like vampires, killing them by sucking their blood. Within 10 years, the otherwise self-sustaining trout population went to zero. Fishermen on Isle Royale reported seeing thousands of fish corpses lying on the lake bottom. The Department of Natural Resources closed the commercial trout fishing season forever.

Because of spectacular efforts by scientists who finally developed a poison to control the lamprey and the departments of Natural Resources who successfully restocked the lake trout, the population came back to normal. A decline in smelt numbers helped the rescue efforts a great deal. But the war isn't won. Too many trout still have fresh lamprey scars, indicating their continued menacing presence.

The chances of seeing another commercial fisherman setting trout nets on McCormick Reef are nil if current resource management plans for Lake Superior remain. Except for a few trout caught by native commercial fishermen and for scientific research, lake trout are now designated as game fish, reserved only for sport fishermen who constitute about 20 percent of the population. The other 80 percent of citizens are not allowed to eat trout unless invited to dinner by a sports fisherman. Our society has decided that lake trout are more valuable as play things than for food.

Wilderness Retreat

After the turn of the 20th century and the dawn of the industrial age, descendants of pioneers were lured from living off the land to the bright lights and security of steady jobs in the city. They left simple, independent lives of wilderness or rural existence for complex lives of dependence on others, where tall buildings, cement and bricks insulated them from nature. Once the newness of city life wore off, some began to miss the advantages of country life.

They missed spectacular sunrises and sunsets, fresh clean air and water, the rich awareness of changing seasons and the joy of providing for their own needs off the land. They needed relief from pressure and stress of hectic, fast-paced, crowded metropolitan living.

Some retreated to the wilderness, part time, by acquiring rustic vacation lake cabins and country homes. Some folks, like Dorothy Molter, Benny Ambrose, Art Madsen, the Powell family, Erv and Tempest Benson, returned to the wilderness permanently. They built log houses on the rocky waters, where they lived off fish, game, gardens, trapping and guiding.

A wilderness retreat has always been part of my life. I can't imagine living without one. During the 1930s and '40s, I was fortunate to grow up experiencing a pioneer lifestyle on Isle Royale in the summer and city living in Duluth during the school season. For 25 years as a commercial artist in Duluth, I was able to keep my wilderness retreat needs alive at Isle Royale and at our log deer shack in the woods. Today we have a cabin/studio at Pine Bay on Lake Superior where I fish, hunt and paint from May to November each year. Elaine and I go south to Grand Marais, Minnesota, to paint in our studio there during winter months.

The ideal wilderness retreat of my imagination is fashioned after Dorothy Molter's cabin on Knife Lake, Benny Ambrose's log cabin on Otter Track, Sig Olson's cabin on Listening Point and my family home on Isle Royale. It looks like the painting – a log cabin built on the edge of a crystal clear lake that provides water, fish, ducks and transportation. The forest behind the cabin provides firewood, garden plot, berries, wild game and pleasant smells.

Odors of wood smoke, baking bread, frying venison and perking coffee on the back stove lid gives me that feeling of well-being that I get nowhere else.

HAPPY BIRTHDAY, JEFF
WITH LOVE....DAD

H. Swertson
©1994

The Deer Shack Connection

In 1492, Columbus discovered a new world with an old history. Shortly after, the fur trade began far to the north and by the 1700s had reached Lake Superior. The recorded history of the Lake Superior region is only 300 years old. I've heard that many of the buildings in England are older than that. Although the fur trade made the local native people dependent on trade goods, they remained hunter-gatherers, living off the land. Hunting, fishing, wild ricing and maple sugar gathering were necessary for their survival until the 20th century.

Early white settlers along the shore were, in a way, hunter-gatherers, too. Although they stayed in one place and raised some of their own food, hunting and fishing were necessary for their survival. They lived close to and understood the working of the natural world and had to obey her laws to survive.

Our modern lifestyles are growing more remote from natural ways. Many do not understand where food comes from. Milk comes from cartons and meat comes in packages at the giant superstore in the mall. Some folks have forgotten that people must kill other animals if they want bacon, steak and chicken on the table.

I was raised in a small commercial fishing community at Isle Royale, where my family's survival depended on catching fish from Lake Superior. If we wanted meat in the fall, a moose was killed and shared with our neighbors. Working outdoors surrounded by wilderness and Lake Superior was, to me, the natural way to live. But I left that way to "better myself" and became a commercial (graphic) artist.

From then on, the best hours of my day in the prime years of my life were spent in a city, in a large building, in a room without windows where I was confined to a four-square-foot drawing board, on which I tried to design advertising messages to influence folks to throw out their old stuff and buy new stuff. My life's work, at that point, was to promote the consumerism our economy depends on to survive. "Shop 'til you drop – or die."

My only connections to the natural world I had left as a young man were vacations spent on Isle Royale and the deer shack Earl Seymour and I built in the middle of 100 square miles of the best deer country in northeastern Minnesota. Earl, his son, Tom, my son, Jeff, and I built the log cabin shown in the painting about 30 years ago. It replaced our first shack built on the same property in 1957. We cut and peeled the logs, erected the cabin and drove a well. Roofing, windows, stoves, tables, chairs, bunks and all the rest of the stuff needed in the shack were hauled in on our backs or on sleds.

We tracked our deer for miles, waiting for the safe, sure shot. By the time we gutted it, dragged it a mile or two to the shack, hung it on the meat pole and cleaned the carcass, we'd become well acquainted with the animal and the consequences of killing it. We experienced the thrill of the hunt and the remorse after taking its life. I understand why Native Americans apologized to their prey and gave thanks to it for its sacrifice.

We also experienced that feeling of well-being as the smell of venison liver frying with onions on the wood cook stove and the sound of fire crackling in the barrel stove mixed with endless tales of the hunts of today and yesterday told around the oak table under the hissing gas lantern.

The whole experience of the deer shack brings me back to a time when we were more self-reliant and knew how to live with the wilderness. Oh, that we could all benefit from that.

If we gain nothing else from hearing about our history, it is that the lives of others give us experience we can use.

Afterword

An artist friend once had an adage posted in her studio: *Art is not a thing, it is a way.*

The fellow who made this book feels the same way. His work is faithful to the view that art should communicate first, decorate second.

Let me call him Buddy. It's how we knew him in Helen Smith's kindergarten room at Jerome Merritt School in West Duluth. We realized his name was Howard, because that's what Miss Smith said, but we stuck with Buddy. I think he likes the nickname. When he grew up he named one of his boats *Buddy Boy*.

We don't know exactly how he found his talent. Art was Buddy's father, but that's the only sign his genes held any bent for drawing and painting. During Ruth Trieglaff's sixth grade Buddy painted nursery rhyme scenes on the walls of the Merritt school library. But when we were on police-boy duty he never talked about vocations – just girls, the trials of school and the fun he had in summer at "the Island."

Like much of his previous work, this book sheds some light on Buddy's growing up and formative years as an artist. The reader benefits, learning how experiences of life and work have influenced his art, his convictions, candor and dedication to salvaging images of an obscure prior time.

Unlike Eastman Johnson, whose subjects posed for him, Buddy had to take a paleological approach to painting the stories he imagined – more like Frances Anne Hopkins, whose work he has always admired. Only painstaking investigation could give him the confidence to put a celluloid collar on Douglass Houghton, or show hivernant voyageurs shouldering canoes at the keel instead of upside down as we do today.

Buddy tends to lament his years as an advertising artist, and we all regret that he wasn't producing more lasting work during that time. Still, those years weren't wasted. He learned discipline. His values jelled. He didn't risk defeat early in his career as many aspiring young creative people do. He learned about the marketplace and that the best recognition an artist can win is to be paid for a painting. He accepted responsibilities to his family, which has now become not only a gratification, but an important asset. He worked for wages when they needed each other most.

Then he and the kids became independent at about the same time. Painters aren't the only ones who begin by being practical. Writers and photographers start out working for newspapers. Musicians teach. Artists conceive ads and brochures to feed their families and pay the rent.

Besides, as many successful artists will tell you, fine art can be more oppressive and commercial than commercial art. Such artists do well by responding to the market, and often find that the market's interest has narrowed to ducks or nostalgia. Buddy has found the integrity to paint his ideas his way and still have a pickup truck that isn't rusty and a couple of skiffs that are paid for.

Today Buddy the Survivor has become Buddy the Educator. His curiosity about this region's cultural roots is keener than ever. His faithful interpretation of old journals and records is filling a vacuum that only a few scholars knew was there. His stories enrich his pictures. His pictures are seasoned (but not revised or distorted) with just enough romanticism to make them worthy of binding into books people will want to own and share. The books provide recognition, which in turn stirs acceptance, making a market for originals and prints. The growing popularity of Buddy's work will reward future generations with a valuable historical resource.

Besides, he's not finished. Like Tennyson's Ulysses, Buddy is a part of all that he has met, and this means his canvas isn't full. There'll be at least one more book before Buddy finally figures out that he can relax a bit more and move into yet another phase of his life as a conservator and communicator. Right now, he thinks the next one will be more autobiographical. Trying to speak for his audience, we trust you, Buddy, and will welcome your ideas, because we agree with our mutual friend Roberta, who reminds us that *art is not a thing, it is a way*.

– Donn Larson
Cloud Bay, Ontario
July 2001

For Further Reading

Pioneers in the Wilderness
by Willis Raff
1981 Cook County Historical Society

The Long Ships Passing
by Walter Havighurst
1961 MacMillon

Lake Superior Indians
By Eastman Johnson and Patricia Johnston
1983 Johnston Publishing

Shepherd of the Wilderness
by Bernard J. Lambert
1967 Bernard J. Lambert

Lake Superior
by Grace Lee Nute
1944 Bobbs-Merrill Company
Re-issued 2000 Minnesota Historical Society Press

William Armstrong
1996 Thunder Bay Art Gallery & Thunder Bay Historical Museum

The West
by Geoffrey C. Ward
1996 The West Book Project Inc.

Chippewa Customs
by Frances Densmore
1979 Minnesota Historical Society Press

Kitchi-Gami
by Johann Georg Kohl
1985 Minnesota Historical Society Press

History of the Ojibway People
by William W. Warren
1984 Minnesota Historical Society Press

Isle Royale
by Thomas P. Gale and Kendra L. Gale
1995 Isle Royale Natural History Association, Houghton, Michigan

Dr. Julius F. Wolff Jr.'s Lake Superior Shipwrecks
by Dr. Julius F. Wolff Jr.
1990 Lake Superior Port Cities Inc.

North of Lake Superior
Charles W. Penny
1970 Marquette County (Michigan) Historical Society

Fort William Post Journals 1821-1870

Lettres des Nouvelle Missions du Canada 1843-1852
Grand Portage National Monument

The Grand Portage Story
by Carolyn Gilman
1992 Minnesota Historical Society Press

Other publications of Lake Superior Port Cities Inc.

Tales of the Old North Shore by Howard Sivertson
  Hardcover: ISBN 0-942235-29-0

The Illustrated Voyageur by Howard Sivertson
  Hardcover: ISBN 0-942235-43-6

Julius F. Wolff Jr.'s Lake Superior Shipwrecks
  Hardcover: ISBN 0-942235-02-9
  Softcover: ISBN 0-942235-01-0

Haunted Lakes (the original) by Frederick Stonehouse
  Softcover: ISBN 0-942235-30-4

Haunted Lakes II by Frederick Stonehouse
  Softcover: ISBN 0-942235-39-8

Shipwreck of the Mesquite by Frederick Stonehouse
  Softcover: ISBN 0-942235-10-x

Wreck Ashore, The United States Life-Saving Service on the Great Lakes
  by Frederick Stonehouse
  Softcover: ISBN 0-942235-22-3

Betty's Pies Favorite Recipes by Betty Lessard
  Softcover: ISBN 0-942235-50-9

The Night the Fitz *Went Down* by Hugh E. Bishop
  Softcover: ISBN 0-942235-37-1

By Water and Rail: A History of Lake County, Minnesota
  by Hugh E. Bishop
  Hardcover: ISBN 0-942235-48-7
  Softcover: ISBN 0-942235-42-8

Shipwrecks of Lake Superior by James R. Marshall
  Softcover: ISBN 0-942235-00-2

Lake Superior Journal: Views from the Bridge by James R. Marshall
  Softcover: ISBN 0-942235-40-1

Michigan Gold, Mining in the Upper Peninsula by Daniel R. Fountain
  Softcover: ISBN 0-942235-15-0

Shipwrecks of Isle Royale National Park by Daniel Lenihan
  Softcover: ISBN 0-942235-18-5

Superior Way, Third Edition by Bonnie Dahl
  Softcover: ISBN 0-942235-49-5

Lake Superior Magazine (Bimonthly)

Lake Superior Travel Guide (Annual)

Lake Superior Wall Calendar (Annual)

Lake Superior Wall Map & Placemats

For a catalog of the entire Lake Superior Port Cities collection
of books and merchandise, write or call:

Lake Superior Port Cities Inc.
P.O. Box 16417 • Duluth, MN 55816
1-888-BIG LAKE (244-5253)
218-722-5002 • FAX 218-722-4096
E-mail: *guide@lakesuperior.com*
www.lakesuperior.com